Mastering AWS CloudFormation

Plan, develop, and deploy your cloud infrastructure effectively using AWS CloudFormation

Karen Tovmasyan

BIRMINGHAM—MUMBAI

Mastering AWS CloudFormation

Commissioning Editor: Vijin Boricha

Acquisition Editor: Meeta Rajani

Senior Editor: Arun Nadar

Content Development Editor: Pratik Andrade

Technical Editor: Dinesh Pawar

Copy Editor: Safis Editing

Project Coordinator: Neil Dmello

Proofreader: Safis Editing

Indexer: Rekha Nair

Production Designer: Nilesh Mohite

First published: May 2020

Production reference: 1070520

Published by Packt Publishing Ltd.
Livery Place
35 Livery Street
Birmingham
B3 2PB, UK.

ISBN 978-1-78913-093-5

www.packt.com

To my mother, Susanna, and my father, Andranik, for everything they did for me. To my wife, Natalia, for being my beloved muse.

- Karen Tovmasyan

Packt.com

Subscribe to our online digital library for full access to over 7,000 books and videos, as well as industry leading tools to help you plan your personal development and advance your career. For more information, please visit our website.

Why subscribe?

- Spend less time learning and more time coding with practical eBooks and Videos from over 4,000 industry professionals

- Improve your learning with Skill Plans built especially for you

- Get a free eBook or video every month

- Fully searchable for easy access to vital information

- Copy and paste, print, and bookmark content

Did you know that Packt offers eBook versions of every book published, with PDF and ePub files available? You can upgrade to the eBook version at packt.com and as a print book customer, you are entitled to a discount on the eBook copy. Get in touch with us at customercare@packtpub.com for more details.

At www.packt.com, you can also read a collection of free technical articles, sign up for a range of free newsletters, and receive exclusive discounts and offers on Packt books and eBooks.

Contributors

About the author

Karen Tovmasyan started his career journey when he was still a student at university. His first job – at one of Renault's factories in Russia – welcomed him and he spent his first year there in IT support, later joining the TechProjects team and having his first servers to manage, which was his first big migration project. A few years later, he joined a SaaS company as a DevOps engineer and in 2016, he moved to the Netherlands. He holds three AWS certifications and is an active member of the Russian-speaking AWS community, helping its members to embrace cloud adoption and make the most of AWS. He gives public talks at conferences and writes content for two personal blogs, on Medium and Telegram.

I want to thank my family, my friends, my readers, and all those who keep learning and improving themselves day after day.

About the reviewers

Anton Tokarev is now working at a company called Softeq with AWS services. He started his career in IT as a network engineer almost 10 years ago. He likes to write code in Python and Go. He has experience with start-ups, big companies, product development companies, and outsourcing.

Aleksandr Patrushev has worked in IT for more than 12 years as a system engineer and public speaker and every new step in his career has been a counterposition to the previous one: from x86 system engineer to IBM Power Systems system engineer at IBM, to VMware system engineer at Vmware, to AWS solution architect at AWS. Each time he jumped out of his comfort zone and ran toward new ideas and technologies. Currently, he is an AWS solution architect who helps companies of any size, from startups to large corporations, through the exciting process of adapting cloud technologies to meet business needs. He loves to find the most efficient solutions for complex projects and challenges. The opinions expressed in the book's review are his own.

I want to say thank you to the author of this book, Karen Tovmasyan, who decided to spend his time creating an interesting book that will help people to understand how to implement the IaC approach in simple language with examples.

Packt is searching for authors like you

If you're interested in becoming an author for Packt, please visit `authors.packtpub.com` and apply today. We have worked with thousands of developers and tech professionals, just like you, to help them share their insight with the global tech community. You can make a general application, apply for a specific hot topic that we are recruiting an author for, or submit your own idea.

Table of Contents

Section 2: Provisioning and Deployment at Scale

3

Validation, Linting, and Deployment of the Stack

4

Continuous Integration and Deployment

5
Deploying to Multiple Regions and Accounts Using StackSets

6
Configuration Management of the EC2 Instances Using cfn-init

Section 3: Extending CloudFormation

7
Creating Resources outside AWS Using Custom Resources

8

Dynamically Rendering the Template Using Template Macros

9

Generating CloudFormation Templates Using AWS CDK

10

Deploying Serverless Applications Using AWS SAM

11
What's Next?

Assessments

Other Books You May Enjoy

Preface

Released in 2011, AWS CloudFormation was the first response to **infrastructure as code** – an emerging approach to managing modern applications, systems, and servers.

In this book, you will learn how to apply Infrastructure-as-Code on AWS using CloudFormation in the most effective way.

By the end of this book, you will have learned about all of the internals of CloudFormation, how it is used in practice, related best practices, and various ways to extend its features using template macros and custom resources.

You will also learn about its alternative for serverless applications – the Serverless Application Model, and its possible future successor – Cloud Development Kit.

Who this book is for

This book is for engineers who work with AWS on a daily basis. Although you will find broad and deep explanations for most of the examples and code blocks in the book, I expect you to have basic knowledge of programming (preferably Python), general IT knowledge, and especially of AWS, as well as an understanding of RESTful APIs, JSON, and YAML.

What this book covers

Chapter 1, CloudFormation Refresher, reminds you what CloudFormation is and how it works.

Chapter 2, Advanced Template Development, covers every single piece of a template – a core component of CloudFormation.

Chapter 3, Validation, Linting, and Deployment of the Stack, teaches you about best practices for stack operations, from validation to running the stack in production.

Chapter 4, Continuous Integration and Deployment, covers another concept of Continuous Delivery and how it is applied with CloudFormation.

Chapter 5, Deploying to Multiple Regions and Accounts Using StackSets, explains how to manage stacks in a multi-region and multi-account environment.

Chapter 6, Configuration Management of the EC2 Instances Using cfn-init, explains how to install software and apply configuration management on EC2 instances using CloudFormation.

Chapter 7, Creating Resources outside AWS Using Custom Resources, explains how to create resources outside of CloudFormation.

Chapter 8, Dynamically Rendering the Template Using Template Macros, covers macros – an advanced concept of CloudFormation – and their use cases.

Chapter 9, Generating CloudFormation Templates Using AWS CDK, introduces Cloud Development Kit – a framework supporting multiple languages that is used to generate CloudFormation templates and operate stacks.

Chapter 10, Deploying Serverless Applications Using AWS SAM, teaches you how to provision resources for serverless applications using the Serverless Application Model – a simplified implementation of CloudFormation.

Chapter 11, What's Next?, gives a sneak peek of what we can expect from the future of Infrastructure-as-Code.

To get the most out of this book

In order to write and test the code in this book, you will need a Linux, macOS, or Windows machine with WSL (Windows Subsystem for Linux). You will need AWS CLI, Python, and obviously an AWS account. You can use any IDE or code editor you prefer. To write the code for this book, I used JetBrains PyCharm and Visual Studio Code, since they have nice plugins for CloudFormation.

For the CDK and SAM, you will additionally need Docker, Homebrew, and **Node package manager** (**NPM**).

All code examples were written on macOS, but they can easily run on a Linux system or WSL.

Software/Hardware covered in the book	OS Requirements
AWS CLI 1.18 or later	macOS and Linux (any)
Python 3.6 or later	macOS, Linux (any), Windows
Homebrew 2.2 or later	macOS, Linux (any), Windows
Docker 19.03.5 or later	macOS, Linux (any), Windows

If you are using the digital version of this book, we advise you to type the code yourself or access the code via the GitHub repository (link available in the next section). Doing so will help you avoid any potential errors related to the copy/pasting of code.

Keep in mind that using CloudFormation on AWS is free but you will pay for the resources it creates. In the book, I tried to use the smallest amount of resources possible (such as t2.micro *instances), but always pay attention to your AWS account and don't forget to delete the stack and other resources once you are done practicing.*

Download the example code files

You can download the example code files for this book from your account at www. packt.com. If you purchased this book elsewhere, you can visit www.packtpub.com/support and register to have the files emailed directly to you.

You can download the code files by following these steps:

1. Log in or register at www.packt.com.
2. Select the **Support** tab.
3. Click on **Code Downloads**.
4. Enter the name of the book in the **Search** box and follow the onscreen instructions.

Once the file is downloaded, please make sure that you unzip or extract the folder using the latest version of:

- WinRAR/7-Zip for Windows
- Zipeg/iZip/UnRarX for Mac
- 7-Zip/PeaZip for Linux

The code bundle for the book is also hosted on GitHub at https://github.com/PacktPublishing/Mastering-AWS-CloudFormation. If there's an update to the code, it will be updated on the existing GitHub repository.

We also have other code bundles from our rich catalog of books and videos available at https://github.com/PacktPublishing/. Check them out!

Code in Action

Code in Action videos for this book can be viewed at https://bit.ly/2YhpSx0.

Download the color images

We also provide a PDF file that has color images of the screenshots/diagrams used in this book. You can download it here: `https://static.packt-cdn.com/downloads/9781789130935_ColorImages.pdf`.

Conventions used

There are a number of text conventions used throughout this book.

`Code in text`: Indicates code words in text, database table names, folder names, filenames, file extensions, pathnames, dummy URLs, user input, and Twitter handles. Here is an example: "We also specify the `AWS::AccountId` pseudo parameter because for the next section, we will deploy the StackSet in multiple regions but in the same account, so we won't need to expose the AWS account ID in the template."

A block of code is set as follows:

```
import boto3
def check_if_key_exists():
    client = boto3.client('ec2')
    try:
        resp = client.describe_key_pairs(KeyNames=["mykey"])
    except Exception:
        return False
    if len(resp['KeyPairs']) == 0:
        return False
    return True
```

Any command-line input or output is written as follows:

```
aws cloudformation deploy \
                --stack-name tag \
                --template-file tag.yaml \
                --capabilities CAPABILITY_IAM
```

Bold: Indicates a new term, an important word, or words that you see onscreen. For example, words in menus or dialog boxes appear in the text like this. Here is an example: "Once both stack instances are created, we will see that their **Status** is **CURRENT** in the **Stack instances** section."

> Tips or important notes
> Appear like this.

Get in touch

Feedback from our readers is always welcome.

General feedback: If you have questions about any aspect of this book, mention the book title in the subject of your message and email us at customercare@packtpub.com.

Errata: Although we have taken every care to ensure the accuracy of our content, mistakes do happen. If you have found a mistake in this book, we would be grateful if you would report this to us. Please visit www.packtpub.com/support/errata, selecting your book, clicking on the Errata Submission Form link, and entering the details.

Piracy: If you come across any illegal copies of our works in any form on the Internet, we would be grateful if you would provide us with the location address or website name. Please contact us at copyright@packt.com with a link to the material.

If you are interested in becoming an author: If there is a topic that you have expertise in and you are interested in either writing or contributing to a book, please visit authors.packtpub.com.

Reviews

Please leave a review. Once you have read and used this book, why not leave a review on the site that you purchased it from? Potential readers can then see and use your unbiased opinion to make purchase decisions, we at Packt can understand what you think about our products, and our authors can see your feedback on their book. Thank you!

For more information about Packt, please visit packt.com.

Section 1: CloudFormation Internals

In our first section, we will do a small refresher on CloudFormation. Later, we will dive deep into its core component – a template – and learn how to write universal, redundant, and reusable templates.

This section comprises the following chapters:

- *Chapter 1, CloudFormation Refresher*
- *Chapter 2, Advanced Template Development*

1
CloudFormation Refresher

Cloud computing introduced a brand-new way of managing the infrastructure.

As the demand for the AWS **cloud** grew, the usual routine and operational tasks became troublesome. The AWS cloud allowed any type of business to rapidly grow and solve all the business needs regarding compute power; however, the need to maintain a certain stack of resources was hard.

DevOps culture brought a set of methodologies and ways of working, and one of those is called **infrastructure as code**. This process is about treating your infrastructure—network, virtual machines, storages, databases, and so on—as a computer program.

AWS **CloudFormation** was developed to solve this kind of problem.

You will already have some working knowledge of CloudFormation, but before we dive deep into learning advanced template development and how to provision at scale, use CloudFormation with CI/CD pipelines, and extend its features, let's quickly refresh our memory and look again at what CloudFormation is and how we use it.

In this chapter, we will learn the following:

- The internals of AWS CloudFormation
- Creating and updating a CloudFormation stack
- Managing permissions for CloudFormation
- Detecting unmanaged changes in our stack

Technical requirements

The code used in this chapter can be found in the book's GitHub repository at `https://github.com/PacktPublishing/Mastering-AWS-CloudFormation/tree/master/Chapter1`.

Check out the following video to see the Code in Action:

`https://bit.ly/2WbU5Lh`

Understanding the internals of AWS CloudFormation

AWS services consist of three parts:

- API
- Backend
- Storage

We interact with AWS by making calls to its API services. If we want to create an EC2 instance, then we need to perform a call, `ec2:RunInstances`.

When we develop our template and create a stack, we invoke the `cloudformation:CreateStack` API method. AWS CloudFormation will receive the command along with the template, validate it, and start creating resources, making API calls to various AWS services, depending on what we have declared for it.

If the creation of any resource fails, then CloudFormation will roll back the changes and delete the resources that were created before the failure. But if there are no mistakes during the creation process, we will see our resources provisioned across the account.

If we want to make changes to our stack, then all we need to do is update the template file and invoke the `cloudformation:UpdateStack` API method. CloudFormation will then update only those resources that have been changed. If the update process fails, then CloudFormation will roll the changes back and return the stack to the previous, healthy, state.

Now that we have this covered, let's start creating our stack.

Creating your first stack

I'm sure you've done this before.

We begin by developing our template first. This is going to be a simple S3 bucket. I'm going to use **YAML** template formatting, but you may use **JSON** formatting if you wish:

MyBucket.yaml

```yaml
AWSTemplateFormatVersion: "2010-09-09"
Description: This is my first bucket
Resources:
  MyBucket:
    Type: AWS::S3::Bucket
```

Now we just need to create the stack with `awscli`:

```
$ aws cloudformation create-stack \
                --stack-name mybucket\
                --template-body file://MyBucket.yaml
```

After a while, we will see our bucket created if we go to the AWS console or run `aws s3 ls`.

Now let's add some public access to our bucket:

MyBucket.yaml

```yaml
AWSTemplateFormatVersion: "2010-09-09"
Description: This is my first bucket
Resources:
  MyBucket:
```

```
  Type: AWS::S3::Bucket
  Properties:
    AccessControl: PublicRead
```

Let's run the `update` operation:

```
$ aws cloudformation update-stack \
                    --stack-name mybucket \
                    --template-body file://MyBucket.yaml
```

To clean up your workspace, simply delete your stack using the following command:

```
$ aws cloudformation delete-stack --stack-name mybucket
```

Let's now look at the CloudFormation IAM permissions.

Understanding CloudFormation IAM permissions

We already know that CloudFormation performs API calls when we create or update the stack. Now the question is, does CloudFormation have the same powers as a *root* user?

When you work with production-grade AWS accounts, you need to control access to your environment for both humans (yourself and your coworkers) and machines (build systems, AWS resources, and so on). That is why controlling access for CloudFormation is important.

By default, when the user runs stack creation, they invoke the API method `cloudformation:CreateStack`. CloudFormation will use that user's access to invoke other API methods during the stack creation.

This means that if our user has an IAM policy with an allowed action `ec2:*`, but attempts to create an RDS instance with CloudFormation, the stack will fail to create with an error, `User is unauthorized to perform this action`.

Let's try this. We will create an IAM role with `ec2:*`, assume that role, and try to create the same bucket stack:

> **Important note**
>
> We already have an IAM user `Admin` in our AWS account and we will add that user as a principal.

MyIamRole.yaml

```yaml
AWSTemplateFormatVersion: "2010-09-09"
Description: "This is a dummy role"
Resources:
  IamRole:
    Type: AWS::IAM::Role
    Properties:
      AssumeRolePolicyDocument:
        Version: 2012-10-17
        Statement:
          - Sid: AllowAssumeRole
            Effect: Allow
            Principal:
              AWS:
                - !Join
                  - ""
                  - - "arn:aws:iam::"
                    - !Ref "AWS::AccountId"
                    - ":user/Admin"
            Action: "sts:AssumeRole"
      ManagedPolicyArns:
        - "arn:aws:iam::aws:policy/AmazonEC2FullAccess"
        - "arn:aws:iam::aws:policy/AWSCloudformationFullAccess"
Outputs:
  IamRole:
    Value: !GetAtt IamRole.Arn
```

If we create this stack, assume that role, and try to create the previous mybucket stack, it will fail to create with an error. Let's take a look:

```
$ aws cloudformation create-stack \
                  --stack-name iamrole \
                  --capabilities CAPABILITY_IAM \
                  --template-body file://IamRole.yaml
```

```
$ IAM_ROLE_ARN=$(aws cloudformation describe-stacks \
                                --stack-name iamrole \
--query "Stacks[0].Outputs[?OutputKey=='IamRole'].OutputValue" \
--output text)
$ aws sts assume-role --role-arn $IAM_ROLE_ARN \
                     --role-session-name tmp
# Here goes the output of the command. I will store the access
credentials in the env vars
$ export AWS_ACCESS_KEY_ID=…
$ export AWS_SECRET_ACCESS_KEY=…
$ export AWS_SESSION_TOKEN=…
$ aws cloudformation create-stack \
                   --stack-name mybucket \
                   --template-body file://MyBucket.yaml
```

We will see the following error on the AWS console:

Logical ID	Status	Status reason
mybucket	⊗ ROLLBACK_COMPLETE	-
MyBucket	⊘ DELETE_COMPLETE	-
mybucket	⊗ ROLLBACK_IN_PROGRESS	The following resource(s) failed to create: [MyBucket]. . Rollback requested by user.
MyBucket	⊗ CREATE_FAILED	API: s3:CreateBucket Access Denied
MyBucket	ⓘ CREATE_IN_PROGRESS	-
mybucket	ⓘ CREATE_IN_PROGRESS	User Initiated

Figure 1.1 – CloudFormation console – stack events

On the other hand, we cannot provide everyone with an AdminAccess policy, so we need to find a way to use CloudFormation with the necessary permissions while only letting CloudFormation use those permissions.

CloudFormation supports **service roles**. Service roles are the IAM roles that are used by different AWS services (such as EC2, ECS, Lambda, and so on). CloudFormation service roles are used by CloudFormation during stacks and StackSets operations—creation, update, and deletion:

1. Let's create a specific role for CloudFormation:

CfnIamRole.yaml

```yaml
AWSTemplateFormatVersion: "2010-09-09"
Description: "This is a CFN role"
Resources:
  IamRole:
    Type: AWS::IAM::Role
    Properties:
      AssumeRolePolicyDocument:
        Version: 2012-10-17
        Statement:
          - Sid: AllowAssumeRole
            Effect: Allow
            Principal:
              Service: "cloudformation.amazonaws.com"
            Action: "sts:AssumeRole"
      ManagedPolicyArns:
        - "arn:aws:iam::aws:policy/AdministratorAccess"
Outputs:
  IamRole:
    Value: !GetAtt IamRole.Arn
```

2. We create this stack for the service role and obtain the CloudFormation role ARN:

```
$ aws cloudformation create-stack \
                --stack-name cfniamrole \
                --capabilities CAPABILITY_IAM \
                --template-body file://CfnIamRole.
yaml
$ IAM_ROLE_ARN=$(aws cloudformation describe-stacks \
```

```
                                                        --stack-name
cfniamrole \
--query "Stacks[0].Outputs[?OutputKey=='IamRole'].
OutputValue" \
--output text)
```

3. Now we run the creation of the stack, which will use our role, specifying the `Role` ARN:

```
$ aws cloudformation create-stack \
                    --stack-name mybucket \
                    --template-body file://MyBucket.yaml
\
                    --role-arn $IAM_ROLE_ARN
```

4. After a while, we can verify that our stack has been created, and we see our bucket!

```
$ aws s3 ls
# Output
2019-10-16 14:14:24 mybucket-mybucket-jqjpr6wmz19q
```

Before we continue, don't forget to clean your account:

```
$ for i in mybucket iamrole cfniamrole; do aws
cloudformation delete-stack --stack-name $i ; done
```

> **Important note**
>
> Note that in the preceding example, we provide the CloudFormation role with an `AdminPolicy` (the one that is provided by AWS by default).

In production-grade systems, we want to allow CloudFormation only those privileges that are required for the stack.

There are two permission schemas that are being applied for CloudFormation roles:

- We have a certain list of services that we can use (for example, EC2, RDS, VPC, DynamoDB, S3, and so on).

- Each template/stack combination will use only those services it needs—for example, if we declare Lambda functions with **Simple Notification Service (SNS)**, then we should create the role with policies only for Lambda and SNS.

Drift detection

CloudFormation as a service often refers to the term **state**. The state is basically inventory information that contains a pair of values: the logical resource name and the physical resource ID.

CloudFormation uses its state to understand which resources to create or update. If we create a stack with a resource with a logical name `foo`, change the property of this resource (`foo`) in a template, and run an update, then CloudFormation will change the corresponding physical resource in the account.

CloudFormation has a set of limitations. For example, it will not update the stack if we do not introduce changes to it. If we perform manual changes to the resource, then CloudFormation will change them only when we make changes to the template.

Developers had to rethink their way of managing the infrastructure once they started using CloudFormation, but we will get to that in the later chapters. For now, we would like to show you a feature that doesn't solve problems of manual intervention, but at least notifies us when they happen. This feature is called drift detection.

For this example, we will use the same template (Dummy IAM Role) as we did in the previous section:

```
$ aws cloudformation create-stack \
                --stack-name iamrole \
                --template-body file://IamRole.yaml \
                --capabilities CAPABILITY_IAM
```

After a while, we see our stack created:

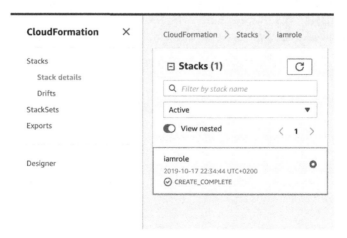

Figure 1.2 – CloudFormation console

Note the link on the right called **Drifts**. If we follow that link, we will see the Drifts menu and under that `Drift status: NOT_CHECKED`. At the time of writing, we will have to run drift detection manually, so we need to run drift detection on our stack. After a while, we will see that everything is all right:

1. I'm going to run `Detect stack drifts` and verify that my stack is compliant:

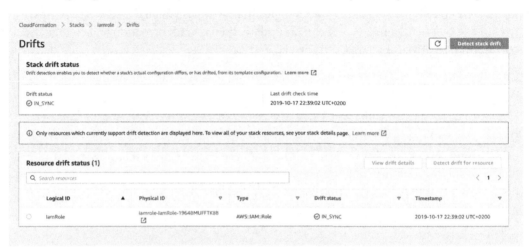

Figure 1.3 – CloudFormation console – drifts

2. Now what we will do is add an extra policy to our role and rerun drift detection:

```
$ ROLENAME=$(aws cloudformation describe-stack-resources
--stack-name iamrole --query "StackResources[0].
PhysicalResourceId" --output text)
```
```
$ aws iam attach-role-policy --role-name
$ROLENAME --policy-arn "arn:aws:iam::aws:policy/
AdministratorAccess"
```

3. We can now detect **drift** again:

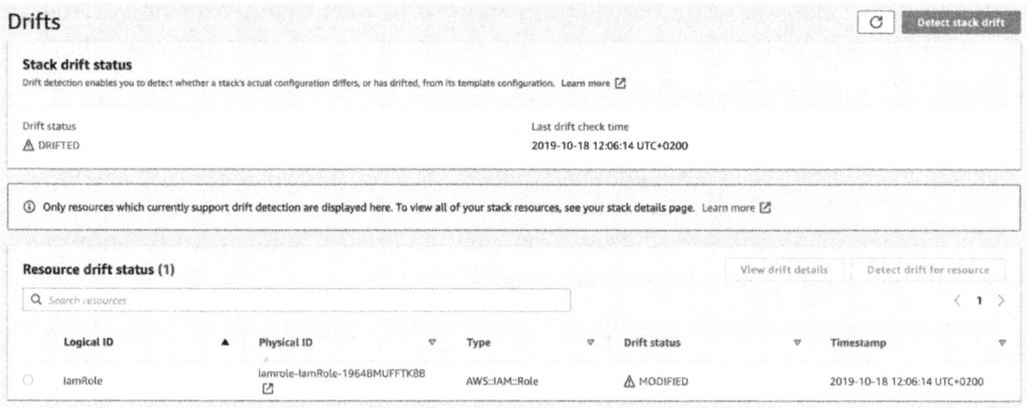

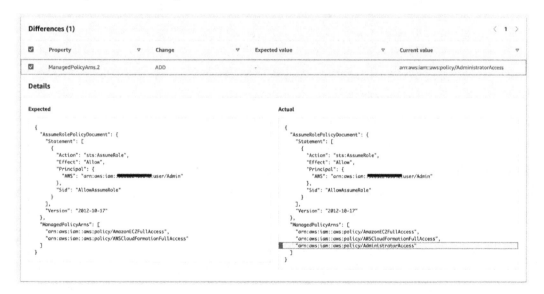

Figure 1.4 – CloudFormation console – drift detected

4. If we check our **IamRole** resource and click on **View drift details**, we will see what exactly has been changed and differs from CloudFormation's state:

Figure 1.5 – CloudFormation console – actual modification

Now we have two options: either roll back the change to the resource manually or add any dummy property to the template and run `update-stack`.

We've learned about CloudFormation drifts, how to run its drift detection, and the actions that must be taken afterward. But don't worry—we will revisit drifts again in the following chapters.

Summary

In this refresher chapter, we refreshed our memory as to what CloudFormation is, how we create and update stacks, why service roles are important, and how to implement them. We also remembered what drifts in CloudFormation are, when they occur, and how to detect them.

While this is an introductory chapter, we covered the fundamental building blocks of CloudFormation. In the following chapters, we will use service roles and drift detection again, but first, we need to deep dive into the internals of the CloudFormation template, which we are going to do in the next chapter.

Questions

1.   Which API method is invoked when we create a CloudFormation stack?

2.   What is a CloudFormation service role?

3.   Which IAM policies are used if we do not specify the CloudFormation service role?

4.   How is the information about stack resources stored in CloudFormation?

5.   What happens if we delete the resource created by CloudFormation and try to create the same stack?

6.   What happens if we delete the resource created by CloudFormation and try to **update** the same stack?

7.   Why can't CloudFormation recreate the deleted resource?

Further reading

- CloudFormation service roles: `https://docs.aws.amazon.com/AWSCloudFormation/latest/UserGuide/using-iam-servicerole.html`

- Drift detection in CloudFormation: `https://docs.aws.amazon.com/AWSCloudFormation/latest/UserGuide/using-cfn-stack-drift.html`

2
Advanced Template Development

Bearing in mind the basics of CloudFormation, let's now move on to advanced development techniques.

In this chapter, we will learn more about the core parts of the CloudFormation templates, and we will do so by building a three-tier application consisting of a web tier (our customer-facing frontend), a middleware tier (processing commands coming from the frontend), and a storage tier (the database where we will store the records).

Don't worry! We're not going to write any software yet (only templates for CloudFormation). For now, we will focus on provisioning our infrastructure.

The following topics will be covered in this chapter:

- Going through the internals of the template
- Creating reusable templates
- Using conditional elements
- Deletion policies
- Referring to existing stacks
- AWS pseudo parameters
- Dynamic references with Parameter Store and Secrets Manager

Technical requirements

The code used in this chapter can be found in the book's GitHub repository at `https://github.com/PacktPublishing/Mastering-AWS-CloudFormation/tree/master/Chapter2`.

Going through the internals of the template

The template is the main building block of CloudFormation. We can consider the template as a declarative instruction for CloudFormation—for example, what to create and how many.

The template file, whether in JSON or YAML, consists of several elements, which we will describe in the rest of this section.

AWSTemplateFormatVersion

The AWSTemplateFormatVersion section is responsible for instructing CloudFormation as to what version of the template we are going to supply it with.

Not to be confused with the API version of CloudFormation, `AWSTemplateFormatVersion` is about the structure of the template.

When AWS has added this block to resolve potential breaking changes to CloudFormation, it can only have one value: `"2010-09-09"`. This version is there from the very beginning of CloudFormation, but there is always a chance that AWS will add newer versions for template formatting. Until then, this section is optional, and if it is not provided, CloudFormation will assume that your template has the default format version mentioned previously.

Description

The description section is optional and serves only one purpose—to explain what your template is and what it is going to create if you push it to CloudFormation. It doesn't allow you to refer to parameters, and supports single-line or multiline values.

Your description can be like this:

```
Description: Core network template consisting of VPC, IGW,
RouteTables, and Subnets
```

It can also be like this:

```
Description: >
Core network template. Consists of:
- VPC
- IGW
- Subnets
- RouteTables
```

There are no specific rules, but keep in mind that unlike comments in your template, the description is also seen in CloudFormation services if you access it via the API, ASW CLI, or AWS Console.

All in all, the best practice for the description is to store useful information for CloudFormation users.

Metadata

While the metadata section might not seem not useful, it adds additional configuration capabilities.

You can use metadata in conjunction with CloudFormation-specific resources, such as the following:

- `AWS::CloudFormation::Init`
- `AWS::CloudFormation::Interface`
- `AWS::CloudFormation::Designer`

We will cover these in more detail later.

Parameters

One of the most important, yet optional, sections, `Parameters`, allows us to make our template reusable. Think of parameters as variables for your stack: CIDR ranges for your VPC and subnets, instance types for your EC2 and RDS instances, and so on.

The use of parameters differs in different cases. One of the most popular ways of using parameters is to allow the creation of different stacks without changing the template resources.

For example, look at the following code:

```
Parameters:
  InstanceType:
    Type: String
Resources:
  Ec2Instance:
    Type: AWS::EC2::Instance
    Properties:
      # ...
      InstanceType: !Ref InstanceType
      # ...
```

In this case, you define the `InstanceType` for your EC2 separately from the actual template, meaning that you can choose different types for different environments (development, testing, production) or other cases.

It is important to know that parameters have the following properties: `Default`, `AllowedValues`, and `AllowedPattern`.

These properties are not mandatory, but it is a best practice to use them.

For example, say that you want to specify the `Environment` tag as a parameter and you have the environments `dev`, `test`, and `prod`. You will likely want to prevent the template user from having to specify the tag that should not be there (such as `foo` or `bar`). For this, you will want to use `AllowedValue`:

```
Parameters:
  Environment:
    Type: String
    AllowedValues: [dev, test, prod]
```

`AllowedPattern` should be used when you want to match your parameter within a specific regular expression. For a case when you need to supply an IP address or a CIDR range, you want to make sure that you will pass exactly the following:

```
Parameters:
  SubnetCidr:
    Type: String
    AllowedPattern: '((\d{1,3})\.){3}\d{1,3}/\d{1,2}'
```

> **Important note**
> You have to make sure that you follow the Java regular expression syntax!

`Default` is a property that helps you to ensure that your parameter always has a value. By design, when you try to create a stack and you don't specify a parameter value, the validation of the template (in the precreation step) will fail.

In this example, we pass a Docker Image tag as a parameter for the ECS Task Definition – Container Definition. To make sure there is an image, we set the default value to `latest` in any case:

```
Parameters:
  DockerImageVersion:
    Type: String
    Default: latest
```

On the other hand, sometimes you need to double check that the template user always knows what they are doing, so it is up to you as a template developer to decide whether you want to have the default values.

Needless to say, parameters have types. The list of types is available on the CloudFormation documentation page at `https://docs.aws.amazon.com/en_pv/AWSCloudFormation/latest/UserGuide/parameters-section-structure`.

One of the most frequently used types is `String`, because most of the property values of `Resources` require this data type, but we can also specify arrays and numbers.

> **AWS-specific parameter types**
> It is handy to use AWS-specific parameter types, such as `AWS::EC2::AvailabilityZone::Name`, `AWS::EC2::Image::Id`, `AWS::EC2::Instance::Id`, `AWS::EC2::KeyPair::KeyName`, and `AWS::EC2::VPC::Id`. The benefit here is that CloudFormation will check whether the value supplied to this specific parameter type is valid for this kind of resource during validation.
>
> For example, if you want to specify the subnet ID as a parameter, you will have to write a correct regular expression for it, while `AWS::EC2::Subnet::Id` already has this check built in.

Mappings

`Mappings` are similar to parameters, but are provided in a dictionary format.

> **Mappings intrinsic functions**
>
> Unlike parameters, whose values are obtained with `Fn::Ref`, values for mappings can be referenced using the `Fn::FindInMap` function.

The most common usage for mappings is when you want to specify the AMI ID for different regions:

```
Mappings:
  RegionMap:
    us-east-1:
      HVM64: ami-0ff8a91507f77f867
      HVMG2: ami-0a584ac55a7631c0c
    us-west-1:
      HVM64: ami-0bdb828fd58c52235
      HVMG2: ami-066ee5fd4a9ef77f1
    eu-west-1:
      HVM64: ami-047bb4163c506cd98
      HVMG2: ami-0a7c483d527806435
    ap-northeast-1:
      HVM64: ami-06cd52961ce9f0d85
      HVMG2: ami-053cdd503598e4a9d
    ap-southeast-1:
      HVM64: ami-08569b978cc4dfa10
      HVMG2: ami-0be9df32ae9f92309
Resources:
  Ec2Instance:
    Type: "AWS::EC2::Instance"
    Properties:
      ImageId: !FindInMap [RegionMap, !Ref "AWS::Region",
HVM64]
```

Note that maintaining mappings can be troublesome, so the best way of using them is to store **constant** values that are rarely changed.

Conditions

Conditions are similar to parameters, but their value is either true or false. Conditions are declared in a separate block in the template and are referred to in the resource declaration.

> **Important note**
>
> Note that Conditions in a declaration cannot be set to true or false manually. The Boolean value is obtained only from a result of intrinsic functions, such as Fn::Equals, Fn::If, Fn::Not, Fn::And, and Fn::Or!

For example, look at the following code:

```
---
AWSTemplateFormatVersion: '2010-09-09'
Parameters:
  Env:
    Default: dev
    Description: Define the environment (dev, test or prod)
    Type: String
    AllowedValues: [dev, test, prod]

Conditions:
  IsProd: !Equals [!Ref Env, 'prod']

Resources:
  Bucket:
    Type: "AWS::S3::Bucket"
    Condition: IsProd
```

In this case, we have to manually provide the Env parameter, which must equal prod; otherwise, the resource will *not* be created.

Conditions work along with specific Boolean intrinsic functions, but those functions also work outside of the conditional block. We will cover these in greater detail when we start the development of our template.

Transform

The transform block is declared when we want to run CloudFormation-specific macros in our template. This is a deep topic that we will cover in the last part of this book, *Extending CloudFormation*

Resources

This is the main and only required block in the `template` file. The resources section provides, as is indicated by its name, resources that we want to provision.

The resources that we create can vary. Some think that any AWS resource can be created by CloudFormation, but there are multiple services (such as AWS Organizations, Control Tower, and many others) that do not support CloudFormation.

Before starting to create the stack, you must first review the resource and property reference in the CloudFormation documentation to make sure that the services you want to use are supported by CloudFormation. For more information, go to https://docs.aws.amazon.com/AWSCloudFormation/latest/ UserGuide/aws-template-resource-type-ref.html.

Resources have multiple attributes, listed as follows:

- **Type**: The type of the resource (instance, subnet, DynamoDB table, lambda function, and so on).

- **Properties**: Configuration of the resource.

- **DependsOn**: Used for adding indirect dependencies.

- **CreationPolicy**: Used for notifying CloudFormation to wait for the signal of completion (we will cover this when we create AutoScaling groups).

- **DeletionPolicy**: Used to instruct CloudFormation what to do with the resource, when we delete it from the stack (or with the stack)—for example, from the *state*. Used for important resources, such as storage backends.

- **UpdatePolicy**: Used to instruct CloudFormation how to handle indirect updates of AutoScaling groups, ElastiCache replication groups, and Lambda function aliases.

- **UpdateReplacePolicy**: Similar to DeletionPolicy, UpdateReplacePolicy is used to manage leftover resources when they have to be replaced with a new one. It works within the same logical resource and default policy as `Delete`.

Outputs

Outputs are the values we *export* from the stack after its creation.

On its own, the outputs do not bring many benefits, but in the previous chapter, we used outputs to automatically get the ARN of the IAM role we created.

Outputs can retrieve the physical name or ID of the resource or its attributes.

For example, we can retrieve the API key and secret for an IAM user when we create it and supply our end users with it:

```
Resources:
  Bob:
    Type: AWS::IAM::User
    Properties:
      UserName: Bob
  BobApiKey:
    Type: AWS::IAM::AccessKey
    Properties:
      UserName: !Ref Bob

Outputs:
  BobKey:
    Value: !Ref BobApiKey
  BobSecret:
    Value: !GetAtt BobApiKey.SecretAccessKey
```

As you can see, we retrieved Bob's API key and secret and exposed it to the outputs.

> **Important note**
> Note that outputs are accessible to anyone who is authorized to read the stacks' description, so exposing security credentials is a risky operation. In case you need to use outputs for that, make sure that only authorized users will have access to your stacks, even if they are read-only.

Outputs also have a powerful feature called exports. Exports allow the template developer to refer to the existing resources, created in another stack. Using exports is a best practice for large workloads where you often have a shared stack (resources used by many applications) and application-specific stacks.

Now, let's start developing our template. Before proceeding, make sure that you understand all the preceding sections because we will rely on them heavily in the coming sections.

Creating reusable templates

We already know that we are going to deploy a three-tier application, but we're going to have more than three stacks.

The first stack we will create is our core stack.

This stack will consist of the following:

- Network (VPC, subnets, and so on)
- IAM (roles and users)

We will have two environments for our application: test and production. These environments will differ in terms of size, the amount of resources, and security settings.

The code of our templates is going to be huge, so you will only see blocks that are specific for the topic; the entire source code can be found in Packt's repository.

Before we start, let's think about how we are going to organize the template and its parameters. Since we are going to reuse the same template for two different stacks (production and test), we will need to separate the network ranges and use different naming conventions.

In terms of network, our stack will have the following:

- 1 VPC
- 3 public subnets
- 3 WebTier subnets
- 3 middleware subnets
- 3 database subnets
- 1 internet gateway
- 1 NAT gateway
- 1 public route table
- 1 private route table
- 2 IAM roles (for administrators and developers)

These resources will have tags such as Name and Env.

In this case, we want to parametrize the properties for our resources, such as CIDR ranges and tags, so we will have the following parameters:

- VPC CIDR range

- Public subnet 1 CIDR range

- Public subnet 2 CIDR range

- Public subnet 3 CIDR range

- WebTier subnet 1 CIDR range

- WebTier subnet 2 CIDR range

- WebTier subnet 3 CIDR range

- Middleware subnet 1 CIDR range

- Middleware subnet 2 CIDR range

- Middleware subnet 3 CIDR range

- Database subnet 1 CIDR range

- Database subnet 2 CIDR range

- Database subnet 3 CIDR range

- Environment

All these parameters will have a type `String`. Let's write our `Parameters` section:

```
Parameters:
  VpcCidr:
    Type: String
    AllowedPattern: '((\d{1,3})\.){3}\d{1,3}/\d{1,2}'
  PublicSubnetCidr1:
    Type: String
    AllowedPattern: '((\d{1,3})\.){3}\d{1,3}/\d{1,2}'
  PublicSubnetCidr2:
    Type: String
    AllowedPattern: '((\d{1,3})\.){3}\d{1,3}/\d{1,2}'
  PublicSubnetCidr3:
    Type: String
    AllowedPattern: '((\d{1,3})\.){3}\d{1,3}/\d{1,2}'
# And so on...
```

```
DatabaseSubnetCidr1:
  Type: String
  AllowedPattern: '((\d{1,3})\.){3}\d{1,3}/\d{1,2}'
DatabaseSubnetCidr2:
  Type: String
  AllowedPattern: '((\d{1,3})\.){3}\d{1,3}/\d{1,2}'
DatabaseSubnetCidr3:
  Type: String
  AllowedPattern: '((\d{1,3})\.){3}\d{1,3}/\d{1,2}'
Environment:
  Type: String
  AllowedValues: ['prod', 'test']
```

This is it for our core stack. Now, in our resources, we will need to use the intrinsic function Fn::Ref to use the value of the parameter in the resource property. We will also use another intrinsic function, Fn::Join, to concatenate a nice string name for our VPC:

```
Resources:
  Vpc:
    Type: "AWS::EC2::VPC"
    Properties:
      CidrBlock: !Ref 'VpcCidr'
      EnableDnsHostnames: True
      EnableDnsSupport: True
      InstanceTenancy: Default
      Tags:
        - Key: 'Name'
          Value: !Join ['-', [ !Ref 'Environment', 'vpc' ]]
        - Key: 'Env'
          Value: !Ref 'Environment'
```

A similar pattern will be used for the remaining resources.

> **Important note**
>
> The Fn::Ref function can also be used to refer to certain attributes from one resource in the stack to another. In this case, we supply Fn::Ref with the logical name of the resource, instead of the parameter.

In the following example, we use `Fn::Ref` to refer to `VpcId` with the subnet we will create next:

```
PublicSubnet1:
  Type: "AWS::EC2::Subnet"
  Properties:
    CidrBlock: !Ref 'PublicSubnetCidr1'
    VpcId: !Ref Vpc
```

Note that I didn't specify the default values for parameters in the template file. In this case, I'm forced to provide them within the `create-stack` command; otherwise, the validation will not pass.

There are two ways to supply CloudFormation with parameters: as a JSON file or as a positional argument.

For large templates with plenty of parameters, you are advised to use JSON files:

```
[
  {
    "ParameterKey": "...",
    "ParameterValue": "..."
  }
]
```

In our case, it will look like the following:

testing.json

```
[
  {
    "ParameterKey": "Environment",
    "ParameterValue": "Testing"
  },
  {
    "ParameterKey": "VpcCidr",
    "ParameterValue": "10.0.0.0/16"
  },
  {
    "ParameterKey": "PublicSubnetCidr1",
```

```
    "ParameterValue": "10.0.1.0/24"
  },
  {
    "ParameterKey": "PublicSubnetCidr2",
    "ParameterValue": "10.0.2.0/24"
  },
  // And so on...
]
```

When we create a template, we specify the parameter file in the argument:

```
$ aws cloudformaiton create-stack \
                --stack-name core \
                --template-body file://core.yaml \
                --parameters file://testing.json
```

In the case that we have default values and want to make a few changes, we can specify the parameters one by one as positional arguments:

```
$ aws cloudformation create-stack \
                --stack-name core \
                --template-body file://core.yaml \
                --parameters \
ParameterKey="Environment",ParameterValue="Testing"ParameterKey
="VpcCid",ParameterValue="10.0.0.0/16"
```

This is suitable if we have a few parameters, but is too complex for a large set of parameters.

> **Important note**
>
> Parameters are provided as a list and elements are split by spaces. Pay attention to the List type parameters, where you will have to use double backslashes:
>
> ```
> ParameterKey=List,ParameterValue=Element1\\,
> Element2
> ```

Let's make a small change to our parameters. Since we have multiple CIDR ranges for each subnet per tier, let's use `List` parameters instead of `Strings`:

```
Parameters:
  VpcCidr:
    Type: String
    AllowedPattern: '((\d{1,3})\.){3}\d{1,3}/\d{1,2}'
  PublicSubnetCidrs:
    Type: List<String>
    AllowedPattern: '((\d{1,3})\.){3}\d{1,3}/\d{1,2}'
# and so on...
  MiddlewareSubnetCidrs:
    Type: List<String>
    AllowedPattern: '((\d{1,3})\.){3}\d{1,3}/\d{1,2}'
  DatabaseSubnetCidrs:
    Type: List<String>
    AllowedPattern: '((\d{1,3})\.){3}\d{1,3}/\d{1,2}'
  Environment:
    Type: String
    AllowedValues: ['prod', 'test']
```

Since we use lists, we cannot use `Fn::Ref` anymore (technically we can, but we will pass the whole list). Instead, we will use `Fn::Select`:

```
PublicSubnet1:
  Type: "AWS::EC2::Subnet"
  Properties:
  CidrBlock: !Select [0, 'PublicSubnetCidrs']
  VpcId: !Ref Vpc


PublicSubnet2:
  Type: "AWS::EC2::Subnet"
  Properties:
  CidrBlock: !Select [1, 'PublicSubnetCidrs']
  VpcId: !Ref Vpc


PublicSubnet3:
```

```
Type: "AWS::EC2::Subnet"
Properties:
CidrBlock: !Select [2, 'PublicSubnetCidrs']
VpcId: !Ref Vpc
```

We can still use `AllowedPattern`, thereby making sure that we use the correct variables. Now, we need to change our parameters file a bit:

```
{
    "ParameterKey": "PublicSubnetCidr1",
    "ParameterValue": [
      "10.0.1.0/24",
      "10.0.2.0/24",
      "10.0.3.0/24"
    ]
}
```

Looks much better now, right?

On the other hand, it might be tricky and too much effort to specify CIDR ranges one by one, especially when you have lots of subnets. For subnet ranges specifically, we can use an intrinsic function called `Fn::Cidr`.

The `Fn::Cidr` function is used to break bigger subnet ranges into smaller ones. This might sound a bit hard at the beginning, but if you understand how to calculate subnet masks, you will benefit from making your parameter file smaller while keeping the logic you need in the template.

Let's get back to our VPC. We specify the VPC CIDR range in the parameter. Our parameter file should now look like the following:

```
[
  {
    "ParameterKey": "VpcCidr",
    "ParameterValue": "10.0.0.0/16"
  }
]
```

In order to break our big subnet into smaller ones (/24), we need to provide the
Fn::Cidr function with the following arguments:

- **ipBlock**: Our CIDR range.

- **count**: How many CIDR ranges we want to generate.

- **cidrBits**: This will tell CFN which ranges to generate. For a /24 CIDR range, we
  need to specify 8.

We know that we will have nine subnets (three for each public, middleware, and database
subnet), so our intrinsic function will appear as follows:

```
Fn::Cidr:
  - !RefVpcCidr
  - 9
  - 8
```

Or, short form syntax, it will look as follows:

```
!Cidr [ !Ref VpcCidr, 9, 8 ]
```

This function returns a list of CIDR ranges, so we need to combine it with Fn::Select
when we declare our subnets. This is how our template will look:

```
PublicSubnet1:
  Type: "AWS::EC2::Subnet"
  Properties:
  CidrBlock: !Select [0, !Cidr [ !GetAttVpcCidr, 9, 8 ]]
  VpcId: !Ref Vpc


PublicSubnet2:
  Type: "AWS::EC2::Subnet"
  Properties:
  CidrBlock: !Select [1, !Cidr [ !GetAttVpcCidr, 9, 8 ]]
  VpcId: !Ref Vpc


PublicSubnet3:
  Type: "AWS::EC2::Subnet"
  Properties:
  CidrBlock: !Select [2, !Cidr [ !GetAttVpcCidr, 9, 8 ]]
  VpcId: !Ref Vpc
```

Using `Fn::Cidr` will allow you to avoid specifying CIDR ranges in the parameters one by one.

> **Important note**
>
> You should be careful when using this function because it expects you to prepare and design your network really well.
>
> You will use `Fn::Cidr` each time you create a subnet, and each time, you need to make sure that the count of CIDR range blocks is the same; otherwise, you will have a subnetting issue and your stack deployment will fail.
>
> If you are creating a network stack separately, your architecture is well designed, and you know what you are doing, then stick to using `Fn::Cidr`.

We will use parameters and intrinsic functions a lot, but let's now learn about another important feature of CloudFormation, called `Conditions`.

Using conditional elements

We want to have reusable templates, but sometimes we need to create a resource in one case and don't need to create one in another, or perhaps create one with different attributes.

Conditions are handy to solve that kind of problem, and can be used in two ways: to specify the `Condition` under the resource or to use the conditional intrinsic function in the resource properties.

We already know that `Condition` is a strict Boolean variable, which is evaluated by parameters and conditional functions. We have already learned how conditions are used in resource declaration (jump to the *Going through the internals of the template* section if you need a refresher), so let's look at another useful example.

Say that we have an AutoScaling group that is built from a launch template. We expect to have a different load on test and production, so we want to adjust the size of the EC2 instance accordingly. For now, we are happy with *t3.micro* on test and *m5.large* on production.

Since we will only have two environments, we can stick to only one condition—`ProdEnv`. Why? Because, in the resource attribute, we use a condition function, `Fn::If`. We use `Fn::If` as it is quite obvious that it has three inputs: condition, value when `True`, and value when `False`. So, if it's not production, we definitely know it is a test.

Let's develop our template:

```
Parameters:
  Env:
    Type: String
    Default: test
    AllowedValues: [ "test", "prod" ]
      ImageId:
        Type: AWS::SSM::Parameter::Value<AWS::EC2::Image::Id>
        Default: '/aws/service/ami-amazon-linux-latest/amzn2-
ami-hvm-x86_64-gp2'


Conditions:
  IsProd: !Equals [ !Ref Env, "prod" ]


Resources:
  WebLt:
    Type: AWS::EC2::LaunchTemplate
    Properties:
      LaunchTemplateName: web
      LaunchTemplateData:
      ImageId: !Ref ImageId
      InstanceType: !If [ IsProd, m5.large, t3.micro ]
```

The long syntax format for the last line would look like this:

```
InstanceType:
  Fn::If:
    - IsProd
    - m5.large
    - t3.micro
```

The Fn::If function also supports inheritance. If we had three environments (test, staging, and production), then we would need to have different instance types on those environments, and we would need extra conditions and a slightly longer condition function:

```
Conditions:
  IsProd: !Equals [ !Ref Env, "prod" ]
  IsStaging: !Equals [!Ref Env, "stage" ]


Resources:
  WebLt:
    Type: AWS::EC2::LaunchTemplate
    Properties:
      LaunchTemplateName: web
      LaunchTemplateData:
        ImageId: !Ref ImageId
        InstanceType: !If [ IsProd, m5.large, !If [ IsStaging, t3.large, t3.micro ] ]
```

Conditions have various use cases, and most of them show up when you start building a big infrastructure on AWS. While you will often find them handy, keep in mind the limitations and usage examples from this book.

Let's now move to another important topic—deletion policies.

Deletion policies

When we create our stack, we need to make sure that mission-critical resources are protected from accidental deletion.

In some cases, this is enabled by EnableTerminationProtection for services such as EC2 and RDS. S3 buckets, when filled with objects, will fail to delete because they have to be emptied first.

Deletion policies allow you to mitigate this risk within CloudFormation. In addition, deletion policies give you a few more features in addition to basic termination protection.

For example, say that you have created a testing stack that you don't need once the testing phase is finished, but you need the dump of the database (which is actually a snapshot of the RDS instance). Sometimes, you don't want to recreate the same data structure, or the database already has important data that you want to move to the production environment.

Let's see whether deletion policies can help us:

```
Resources:
  VeryImportantDb:
    Type: AWS::RDS::Instance
    DeletionPolicy: Snapshot
    Properties:
      # Here you set properties for your RDS instance.
```

What will happen when we remove this resource from the template or delete the stack is that CloudFormation will signal RDS to take a final snapshot of the instance and then delete it.

> **Important note**
>
> The deletion policy snapshot is not available for every single resource. At the time of writing, the supported resources are
> `AWS::EC2::Volume`, `AWS::ElastiCache::CacheCluster`,
> `AWS::ElastiCache::ReplicationGroup`,
> `AWS::Neptune::DBCluster`, `AWS::RDS::DBCluster`, and
> `AWS::RDS::DBInstance`, `AWS::Redshift::Cluster`.
>
> Bear that in mind when you design your infrastructure.

Another situation is when we want to retain some of the resources when we delete the stack. Here, we use the deletion policy called `Retain`:

```
Resources:
  EvenMoreImportantDb:
    Type: AWS::RDS::Instance
    DeletionPolicy: Retain
    Properties:
      # Here you set properties for your RDS instance.
```

In case of deletion, what will happen is that this DB instance will be removed from CloudFormation's state, but the resource itself will stay in our account.

Another deletion policy is, obviously, `Delete`, which is a default policy for all the resources in the template. If we do not specify any deletion policy for the resource, it will be deleted from the stack or with the stack.

Unfortunately, deletion policies cannot be combined with Conditions, since they only allow the storing of String values. What do we need to do if we want different deletion policies for different conditions?

Well, this will require us to declare the same resource multiple times, but with different logical name, condition, and deletion policies.

We don't have to worry about resource duplication, if we set up conditions properly:

```yaml
Parameters:
  Environment:
    Type: String
    AllowedValued: [ "dev", "test", "prod" ]
    Default: "dev"


Conditions:
  ProdEnv: !Equals [ !Ref Environment, "prod" ]
  TestEnv: !Equals [ !Ref Environment, "test" ]
  DevEnv: !Equals [ !Ref Environment, "dev" ]
```

Then, our Resource section would look like the following:

```yaml
Resources:
  ProdDatabase:
    Condition: ProdEnv
    Type: AWS::RDS::DBInstance
    DeletionPolicy: Retain
    Properties:
      # Properties for production database
  TestDatabase:
    Condition: TestEnv
    Type: AWS::RDS::DBInstance
    DeletionPolicy: Snapshot
    Properties:
      # Properties for test database
  DevDatabase:
    Condition: DevEnv
    Type: AWS::RDS::DBInstance
```

```
    DeletionPolicy: Delete
    Properties:
      # Properties for dev database
```

This introduces extra complexity for our template but makes it more universal.

Protecting your data is important, so always make sure that you use deletion policies for storage services, such as databases, and storage backends, such as S3 buckets or EBS volumes.

Now that we know how to mitigate the risk of data loss, let's move on to the next topic.

Referring to existing stacks

In large environments with shared responsibility models, where different teams manage their own stack resources, we sometimes have a situation that resources or resource attributes (RDS instance endpoints, for example) have to be shared between different stacks.

Remember that we have a network stack in our application. Resources from this stack, such as subnets, are used in the application templates.

Whenever you deploy a virtual machine, AutoScaling group, load balancer, or a database cluster, you need to specify the subnet ID. We can specify that subnet ID as a parameter and then use Fn::Ref to map it in the resource attribute, but that will require a lot of unnecessary actions that can be avoided, by using exports and Fn::ImportValue.

In *Chapter 1, CloudFormation Refresher*, we used outputs to obtain the ARN of the IAM role, which we used in the AWS command line.

Outputs are handy for quickly accessing the attributes of created resources, but they can also be transformed into exports.

Exports are the aliases to the physical resource IDs. Each Export name must be unique within a region, but doesn't have to be within a single account.

This means that when we want to refer to the resource attribute created in another stack, we need to create an output record with the Export name. Once this is done and the stack is created, we can then refer to it using an intrinsic function called Fn::ImportValue.

The Fn::ImportValue function will look up the necessary attribute in the CloudFormation exported values across the whole account within a region and write a necessary entry to the resource attribute.

If this sounds a bit complicated, let's look at how this works in an example. Here, we create subnets in our core stack and we need to use their IDs in our WebTier (and other) stacks. This is what our core template will look like:

core.yaml

```yaml
Parameters:
# ...
Resources:
  Vpc:
    Type: AWS::EC2::VPC
    Properties:
      # ...

  PublicSubnet1:
    Type: AWS::EC2::Subnet
    Properties:
      # ...
  # The rest of our resources...
```

The Outputs section is as follows:

```yaml
Outputs:
  VpcId:
    Value: !Ref Vpc
    Export:
      Name: Vpc
  PublicSubnet1Id:
    Value: !Ref PublicSubnet1
    Export:
      Name: PublicSubnet1Id
  PublicSubnet2Id:
    Value: !Ref PublicSubnet2
    Export:
      Name: PublicSubnet2Id
  PublicSubnet3Id
    Value: !Ref PublicSubnet3
```

```
    Export:
        Name: PublicSubnet3Id
# And so on
```

Here is how we refer to exported values from the core stack:

webtier.yaml

```
Resources:
  WebTierAsg:
    Type: AWS::AutoScaling::AutoScalingGroup
    Properties:
      # Some properties...
      VpcZoneIdentifier:
        - !ImportValue PublicSubnet1Id
        - !ImportValue PublicSubnet2Id
        - !ImportValue PublicSubnet3Id
      # And so on...
```

You've noticed that I'm doing extra work here by creating additional exports and importing those values one by one.

Sometimes, you need to import single attributes, such as a shared secret or an IAM role for ECS task execution, but for listed items, such as subnets or Availability Zones, it is wise to combine them into lists and refer to them as lists.

Let's refactor the preceding example into a simpler structure:

core.yaml

```
Outputs:
  PublicSubnetIds:
    Value: !Split [",", !Join [",", [!Ref PublicSubnet1, !Ref
PublicSubnet2, !Ref PublicSubnet3]  ]  ]
    Export:
      Name: PublicSubnetIds
```

What we do here is that we make a comma-separated string with our subnet IDs and then use Fn::Split to turn this long string into a list. Since there is no intrinsic function to generate a list of elements, we have to use this workaround.

Now, we can import this value in a shorter form:

webtier.yaml

```
Resoures:
  WebTierAsg:
    Type: AWS::AutoScaling::AutoScalingGroup
    Properties:
      # Some properties
      VpcZoneIdentifier: !ImportValuePublicSubnetIds
```

Since we already pass a list of values, CloudFormation will parse it properly and create the instance's AutoScaling group the way we need it.

Outputs/exports also support conditional functions. In the previous section (*Deletion policies*), we had to declare the same DB instance multiple times. If we create exports for each of them, the stack creation will fail because not every single one of them is being created. It is wise to also use conditional functions there.

> **Important note**
>
> Note that outputs do not have the condition attribute, like resources. We have to use conditional functions in order to use the correct value for exports.

database.yaml

```
Outputs:
  DbEndpoint:
    Value: !If [ ProdEnv, !GetAttProdDatabase.Endpoint.Address,
!If [ TestEnv, !GetAttTestDatabase.Endpoint.Address, !GetAtt.
DevDatabase.Endpoint.Address ]]
    Export:
      Name: DbEndpoint
```

This is one of the cases when a short syntax form makes our template almost unreadable, so let's write it in a standard syntax form:

```
Outputs:
  DbEndpoint:
    Value:
      Fn::If:
```

```
            -  ProdEnv
            -  !GetAttProdDatabase.Endpoint.Address
            -  Fn::If:
                -  TestEnv
                -  !GetAttTestDatabase.Endpoint.Address
                -  !GetAttDevDatabase.Endpoint.Address
      Export:
        Name: DbEndpoint
```

Looks much better, right? However, it is up to you to decide which syntax form (long or short) to choose when you declare complex conditional checks. Just don't forget that you write the code not only for the machine (CloudFormation, in our case), but also for your fellow colleagues.

Now, let's move to the next important topic, which is about AWS pseudo parameters.

AWS pseudo parameters

What makes these parameters special? Well, the fact that they are obtained from AWS itself.

The current list of these parameters is as follows:

- AWS::AccountId
- AWS::NotificationARNs
- AWS::NoValue
- AWS::Region
- AWS::StackId
- AWS::StackName
- AWS::URLSuffix
- AWS::Partition

We're not going to cover all of them, only the most widely used ones.

AWS::AccountId

One of the use cases where we need to use AccountId is when we are using an IAM principal.

If you are familiar with IAM, then you know that we can set the AWS account ID as a principal element. If you need to refresh your memory regarding IAM, you can read a great blog series at `https://medium.com/@thomas.storm/aws-iam-deep-dive-chapter-1-essentials-a9cfb1931a01`.

At the same time, it is dangerous to expose your AWS account ID; we should always stick to using AWS pseudo parameters when we specify this kind of sensitive information.

An example usage of `AWS::AccountId` is as follows:

```
Resources:
  MyIamRole:
    Type: AWS::IAM::Role
    Properties:
      AssumeRolePolicyDocument:
        Version: 2012-10-17
        Statement:
          - Effect: Allow
            Action:
              - sts:AssumeRole
            Principal:
              AWS: !Ref "AWS::AccountId"
            Sid: "AllowRoleAssume"
      # The rest of the IAM role properties...
```

As with any other parameter, pseudo parameters can be used in conjunction with intrinsic functions. The following is an example (you probably remember it from *Chapter 1, CloudFormation Refresher*) where we specify all users within an account in `Principal`:

```
  MyIamRole:
    Type: AWS::IAM::Role
    Properties:
      AssumeRolePolicyDocument:
        Version: 2012-10-17
        Statement:
          - Sid: AllowAssumeRole
            Effect: Allow
            Principal:
              AWS:
```

```
          - !Join
            - ""
            - - "arn:aws:iam::"
              - !Ref "AWS::AccountId"
              - ":user/${aws.username}"
        Action: "sts:AssumeRole"
```

Note the ${aws.username} variable. This variable is not a part of CloudFormation, but a part of IAM policy variables.

When we initiate stack deployment, CloudFormation will replace the pseudo parameter with an actual value. For AWS::AccountId, the value will be the account where the stack is being created.

AWS::NoValue

The AWS::NoValue phrase is an equivalent of the *null* value. There is not much practical usage for it, unless you want to combine it with conditional functions. It is important to know that if you supply your resource property with AWS::NoValue, it will act as if you hadn't specified this property at all.

One use case of this would be using it to create a database from a snapshot or from scratch:

```
Resources:
  MyDB:
    Type: AWS::RDS::DBInstance
    Properties:
      AllocatedStorage: "5"
      DBInstanceClass: db.t3.micro
      Engine: MySQL
      EngineVersion: "5.7"
      DBSnapshotIdentifier:
        Fn::If:
          - UseDBSnapshot
          - Ref: DBSnapshotName
          - Ref: AWS::NoValue
```

In the last few lines, we can see that if the condition is not met, then the DBSnapshotIdentifier property will not be used.

AWS::Region

Some resources require you to specify the AWS region. Hardcoding the region might not be a security issue, but will cause us trouble when we deploy the same stack in different regions. It is a best practice to use this pseudo parameter, even if you don't plan to deploy multi-regional applications.

For example, when we create an ECS task definition and want to use CloudWatch logs as a log driver, we need to specify a log group and AWS region:

```
Resources:
  EcsTaskDefinition:
    Type: AWS::ECS::TaskDefinition
    Properties:
      # Some properties...
      ContainerDefinition:
        - Name: mycontainer
          # Some container properties...
          LogConfiguration:
          LogDriver: awslogs
            Options:
              awslogs-group: myloggroup
              awslogs-region: !Ref "AWS::Region"
              awslogs-stream-prefix: ""
```

When this stack is created, CloudFormation will create a CloudWatch log group in the same region where the stack resources were provisioned.

AWS::StackId and AWS::StackName

The AWS::StackId and AWS::StackName pseudo parameters are handy when you need to specify tags for your resources. An example usage is giving an application name to the name of the stack and reusing it in Tags:

```
Resources:
  SomeResource:
    Type: # any, that supports tags
    Properties:
      # Some properties..
```

```
Tags:
   - Key: Application
     Value: !Ref "AWS::StackName"
```

Referring to `AWS::StackName` in the `Tags` value will indicate the CloudFormation stack that this resource belongs to.

AWS::URLSuffix

The `AWS::URLSuffix` pseudo parameter is needed for specifying AWS URLs. In 99% of cases, it's going to be amazonaws.com, but if you plan to deploy your application to a special region, such as China or AWS GovCloud, you will have to use their own URL suffixes.

You need a URL suffix for services such as IAM roles if this role has to be assumed by AWS—for instance, ECS's task execution role:

```
Resources:
  EcsTaskExecutionRole:
    Type: AWS::IAM::Role
    Properties:
      AssumeRolePolicyDocument:
        Version: 2012-10-17
        Statement:
          - Sid: AllowAssumeRole
            Effect: Allow
            Principal:
              Service: !Join ["." [ "ecs-tasks",!Ref
"AWS::URLSuffix" ] ]
            Action: "sts:AssumeRole"
      # Some role properties...
```

Using pseudo parameters will make your template recyclable and flexible. If you have to deploy your application in another region or even account, the amount of refactoring will be minimal.

AWS::Partition

When we need to define an ARN of the resource manually, we often write it in the following manner: `arn:aws:service:region:account_id:...`

The word `aws` here refers to a partition – which we can refer to as a `namespace`. For most of the cases, you will see "aws", but you want to know that there are other partitions as well. For example, regions in China have a partition `aws-cn`, and GovCloud regions have a partition `aws-us-gov`.

This said, let's continue with another important topic – dynamic referencing in the templates.

Let's move on to the last bit of this chapter, which is about using dynamic references for your stacks with AWS SSM Parameter Store and AWS Secrets Manager.

Dynamic references with Parameter Store and Secrets Manager

At the beginning of this chapter, we looked at passing parameters either in a JSON file or as a command-line argument.

Although it is a known practice in infrastructure-as-code to keep parameters in a **version control system** (**VCS**), it introduces additional complexity.

If we store parameters in a VCS, we need to take care of encrypting sensitive data, such as passwords or other credentials. If we pass them via command-line arguments, we have to make sure we don't make a mistake or a typo (which is a common occurrence in the life of IT engineers).

To solve these issues, we can store template parameters in the SSM Parameter Store or Secrets Manager (for passwords).

They both support versioning, so we can always revert the parameters to the previous version if there was a mistake and then redeploy our stack.

Another benefit of using the Parameter Store and Secrets Manager is that we can provide developers who are not responsible for CloudFormation development with the ability to apply slight changes to the stack, such as changing the instance type or increasing the size of the `AutoScaling` group.

What we are going to do now is append our core template with a few parameters for our application templates:

core.yaml

```yaml
Resources:
# Some resources...
  WebAsgMinSize:
    Type: AWS::SSM::Parameter
    Properties:
      Type: String
      Value: "1"
  WebAsgMaxSize:
    Type: AWS::SSM::Parameter
    Properties:
      Type: String
      Value: "1"
  WebAsgDesiredSize:
    Type: AWS::SSM::Parameter
    Properties:
      Type: String
      Value: "1"
# The rest...
```

Then, we will add SSM parameters to the outputs:

```yaml
Outputs:
# Original outputs...
  WebAsgMinSize:
    Value: !Ref WebAsgMinSize
    Export:
      Name: WebAsgMinSize
  WebAsgMaxSize:
    Value: !Ref WebAsgMaxSize
    Export:
      Name: WebAsgMaxSize
  WebAsgDesiredSize:
```

```
        Value: !Ref WebAsgDesiredSize
      Export:
        Name: WebAsgDesiredSize
```

We created three parameters for the web tier stack to use. Now, we need to refer to those parameters in the web tier template. There are two ways we can do this:

- Refer to them from the parameters
- Refer to them from the resource declaration

You will recall that we've used AWS-specific parameters in the parameter section when we were creating our WebTier template (look at the *Using conditional elements* section if you need a refresher).

While the use of this is relatively obvious and simple, this will require us first to create a core stack and then copy and paste the SSM Parameter Store parameter's name to the parameters section in the template.

To reduce the number of manual actions, it is wise to *resolve* the parameter right in the resource declaration.

This is how it works: once the parameter is created and you have its name, you can pass it to a resource property by using Jinja formatting: `"{{resolve:service-name:reference-key}}"`.

We can use the SSM parameter name or ARN.

For our case, we export the parameter's ARN. Let's now resolve it in the web tier `AutoScaling` group resource:

---

webtier.yaml

```
Resources:
# WebTier resources...
  WebTierAsg:
    Type: AWS::AutoScaling::AutoScalingGroup
    Properties:
      # Properties of ASG...
      DesiredCapacity:
        Fn::Join:
          - ":"
          - - "{{resolve:ssm"
```

```
              - !ImportValueWebAsgDesiredSize
            - "1}}"
    MaxSize:
        Fn::Join:
          - ":"
          - - "{{resolve:ssm"
              - !ImportValueWebAsgMaxSize
            - "1}}"
    MinSize:
        Fn::Join:
          - ":"
          - - "{{resolve:ssm"
              - !ImportValueWebAsgMinSize
            - "1}}"
```

In the preceding code, our properties refer not to the template parameters, but to the values of SSM parameters.

> **SSM Parameter Store limitations**
>
> At the time of writing, it is not possible to refer to the latest version of the parameters in the SSM Parameter Store. If you make a change to the parameter, you will still have to change the version of it in the resolve block.

We can use the same method to randomly generate a DB password, so we don't have to hardcode and/or expose it:

database.yaml

```
Resources:
  DbPwSecret:
    Type: AWS::SecretsManager::Secret
    Properties:
      GenerateSecretString:
      GenerateStringKey: "DbPassword"
  RdsInstance:
    Type: AWS::RDS::DBInstance
    Properties:
      # Some RDS Instance properties...
```

```
MasterUserPassword:
    Fn::Join:
        - ":"
        - - "{resolve:secretsmanager"
          - !RefDbPwSecret
          - "SecretString:DbPassword}}"
```

Note that, unlike SSM parameters, we do not specify the secret's version, but the actual key we want to refer to.

Summary

Although we didn't deploy any stacks, we went through every bit of the main building block of CloudFormation in this chapter.

We learned how to make our templates reusable and recyclable, how to control them using conditions, and how to protect stack resources from accidental or intentional deletions. We've also covered dynamic parameter referencing, which we will use more and more toward the end of this book.

Before continuing to the next chapter, make sure you have gone through the templates in the repository and understood each line.

In the next chapter, we will dive into the preflight checks and various ways of provisioning stack resources.

Questions

1. Can we use `Intrinsic` functions in the `Conditions` attribute in `Resource`?
2. Can we use an `Intrinsic` function for conditions in the `Resource` property?
3. What is the difference between `UpdatePolicy` and `UpdateReplacePolicy`?
4. Which *DeletionPolicy* should be used for a mission-critical database?
5. What is `Fn::ImportValue` used from?
6. Is it possible to create multiple exports with the same name?
7. Is there a parameter data type used specifically for AMIs?
8. What is `AWS::NoValue`? What are its use cases?

Further reading

- Template anatomy: `https://docs.aws.amazon.com/AWSCloudFormation/latest/UserGuide/template-anatomy.html`

- Dynamic referencing: `https://docs.aws.amazon.com/AWSCloudFormation/latest/UserGuide/dynamic-references.html`

- Deletion policies: `https://docs.aws.amazon.com/AWSCloudFormation/latest/UserGuide/aws-attribute-deletionpolicy.html`

- Sample templates: `https://docs.aws.amazon.com/AWSCloudFormation/latest/UserGuide/cfn-sample-templates.html`

Section 2: Provisioning and Deployment at Scale

In this section, we are going to practice a lot with CloudFormation stack operations and see how we can apply DevOps practices using CloudFormation and AWS.

This section comprises the following chapters:

- *Chapter 3, Validation, Linting, and Deployment of the Stack*
- *Chapter 4, Continuous Integration and Deployment*
- *Chapter 5, Deploying to Multiple Regions and Accounts Using StackSet*
- *Chapter 6, Configuration Management of the EC2 Instances Using cfn-init*

3
Validation, Linting, and Deployment of the Stack

So far, we have not deployed our stacks yet. While we have learned the features of the template, this knowledge has no value if we do not provision our resources.

This chapter is about the checks we need to perform before provisioning our resources, various ways to deploy the stack, and which steps are being performed.

The following topics will be covered in this chapter:

- Validating the template
- Using a linter for best practices on templates
- Provisioning our stack
- Handling errors
- Working with drifts

Technical requirements

The code used in this chapter can be found in the book's GitHub repository at `https://github.com/PacktPublishing/Mastering-AWS-CloudFormation/tree/master/Chapter3`.

Check out the following video to see the Code in Action:

`https://bit.ly/2Wbjkh1`

Validating the template

Whenever we execute `aws cloudformation create-stack` (or `update-stack`), CloudFormation will first validate the template, checking whether it is a valid JSON or YAML file (a syntax check) and whether there are any critical issues, such as circular dependencies.

Although template validation is a necessary step before stack deployment, there are many things that will break stack deployment even if validation succeeds:

- Missing required resource properties
- Syntax errors and typos in resource property names
- Non-existent resource property values

We could continue with this list, but let's move from theory to practice.

The command that runs template validation is straightforward:

```
$ aws cloudformation validate-template --template-body file://
path_to_your_template
```

For example, if we want to validate our core template, we need to run the following command:

```
$ aws cloudformation validate-template --template-body file://
core.yaml
```

If there is an error in the template, we will see the following output (for this example, I've changed the `PublicSubnet1` resource type to `AWS::EC2::DoesNotExist`):

```
An error occurred (ValidationError) when calling the
ValidateTemplate operation: Template format error: Unrecognized
resource types: [AWS::EC2::DoesNotExist]
```

If we simulate a typo error in an intrinsic function, we will get another error (for this example, I've changed the intrinsic function `Fn::Select` to `Fn::NoSelect`):

```
An error occurred (ValidationError) when calling the
ValidateTemplate operation: Template format error: YAML not
well-formed. (line 31, column 18)
```

However, if the template is valid, we will see the parameters of the template, its description, and IAM capabilities with the reason, which shows the resource that requires it:

```
{
    "Parameters": [
        {
            "ParameterKey": "VpcCidr",
            "NoEcho": false
        },
        {
            "ParameterKey": "Environment",
            "NoEcho": false
        }
    ],
    "Description": "Core template. Contains network and iam
roles",
    "Capabilities": [
        "CAPABILITY_IAM"
    ],
    "CapabilitiesReason": "The following resource(s) require
capabilities: [AWS::IAM::Role]"
}
```

The validator always runs before stack deployment, but in order to save time and catch all the errors as early as possible, you should always consider running validation before deploying the stack and using it as a step in your CI/CD pipeline (which we will cover in the next chapter).

Let's move to an interesting tool called `cfn-lint`.

Using a linter for best practices on templates

Let's describe a linter again. This is how Wikipedia defines a linter:

"Lint, or a linter, is a tool that analyzes source code to flag programming errors, bugs, stylistic errors, and suspicious constructs."

CloudFormation's linter, known as a `cfn-lint`, is a command-line tool that inspects your template and compares the declared resources against a wide range of written rules.

Unlike the template validator, `cfn-lint` can detect tricky issues such as missing resource properties or arguments in an intrinsic function.

CloudFormation's linter is an external tool that can be installed using `pip`:

```
$ pip install cfn-lint
```

It will automatically appear in `$PATH`, so we can run it right away:

```
$ cfn-lint core.yaml
```

If the template meets all the rule requirements, we will see nothing on the output (and the *return code* of the command will be 0). However, if there is an error, the linter will notify us immediately.

For this example, I've commented out the `VpcId` property and removed the mask bits in the `Fn::Cidr` function. The `PublicSubnet2` resource looks like the following:

```
  PublicSubnet2:
    Type: "AWS::EC2::Subnet"
    Properties:
      # Missing argument for mask bits!!!
      CidrBlock: !Select [ 1, !Cidr [ !Ref VpcCidr, 12 ] ]
      #VpcId: !Ref Vpc  # Missing property!
      MapPublicIpOnLaunch: True
      AvailabilityZone: !Select
        - 1
        - Fn::GetAZs: !Ref "AWS::Region"
      Tags:
        - Key: 'Name'
          Value: !Join ['-', [ !Ref 'Environment', 'public-
subnet02' ]]
        - Key: 'Env'
          Value: !Ref 'Environment'
```

This is the output of running the linter:

```
$ cfn-lint core_broken.yaml
E0002 Unknown exception while processing rule E1024: list index
out of range
core.yaml:1:1


E3003 Property VpcId missing at Resources/PublicSubnet2/
Properties
core.yaml:45:5
```

The *return code* will be 1 or 2 (these are common return codes for errors in Linux systems).

> **Important note**
>
> You have noticed that cfn-lint also shows which lines it found a mistake on. However, when you mess around with arguments for intrinsic functions, you will see the error on the first line, which is not the case.
>
> Also, the error is not an actual error pointed to by the linter. This is a Python exception.

The linter doesn't only check our templates against built-in rules, but also supports tweaking and customization.

Linting against specific regions

When you run cfn-lint, it will check your template against the default region (which is us-east-1). In order to check against other regions, you can specify it manually:

```
$ cfn-lint core.yaml --regions 'eu-west-1'
# or...
$ cfn-lint core.yaml --regions 'eu-west-1','us-east1'
# or even...
$ cfn-lint core.yaml --regions 'ALL_REGIONS'
```

In the last example, you will get an even more interesting result:

```
E3001 Invalid or unsupported Type AWS::SSM::Parameter for
resource MiddlewareAsgMaxSizeParameter in us-gov-west-1
core.yaml:393:5
```

```
E3001 Invalid or unsupported Type AWS::SSM::Parameter for
resource MiddlewareAsgMaxSizeParameter in us-gov-east-1
core.yaml:393:5


E3001 Invalid or unsupported Type AWS::SSM::Parameter for
resource MiddlewareAsgMaxSizeParameter in eu-north-1
core.yaml:393:5


E3001 Invalid or unsupported Type AWS::SSM::Parameter for
resource MiddlewareAsgMaxSizeParameter in ap-east-1
core.yaml:393:5
```

This error is triggered because the regions mentioned do not support this resource type. If you plan to deploy your template to various regions, it is wise to include all or a part of them in the check, so you make sure that services and resources you want to provision are actually supported by CloudFormation.

Another way to include regions to be checked against is to add them in the template's metadata:

core.yaml

```
Metadata:
  cfn-lint:
    regions:
      - us-east-1
      - eu-west-1
      - eu-central-1
```

Then, `cfn-lint` will automatically pick these regions when you run the check.

> **Important note**
> Note that the template's metadata values are always overridden by command-line arguments.

Let's see how we can make `cfn-lint` ignore specific rules so we can make it less strict.

Ignoring specific rules

If you include `cfn-lint` in your CI/CD pipeline, you will get into trouble if you mark the step as failed if the return code of the linter is not 0. If `cfn-lint` fires a warning (which is not necessarily an issue) you might want to ignore it if it is not applicable to your stack.

You can ignore specific rules by supplying an `--ignore-checks` argument:

```
cfn-lint core.yaml --ignore-checks 'W2001'
```

Or you can include them in the metadata as well:

```
Metadata:
  cfn-lint:
    regions:
      - us-east-1
      - eu-west-1
      - eu-central-1
    ignore-checks:
      - W2001
```

Ignoring the linter rule though is not recommended, so only use it for specific rules, such as non-existent services, when you lint your template against all regions.

Creating custom rules

`cfn-lint` has a rich library for checks and rules. However, your organization might have its own requirements for templates (such as necessary `Tags`) that do not come out of the box.

`cfn-lint` supports creation of custom rules. Custom rules have to be written in the same language as `cfn-lint` (for example, Python) and need to be appended when the linter is running.

Before we add our custom rules, let's first develop one! Our scenario is that we want to make sure that our RDS resources (such as DB instances and DB clusters) have a `DeletionPolicy`, and that `DeletionPolicy` is **not** set to `Delete`.

Part of the job is already done: `cfn-lint` has a built-in template parser, so we only need to match specific resources and check that they have the required property.

The flow of the linter rule will be the following:

1. The rule will check if there are resources in the template with a type of `AWS::RDS::DBInstance` or `AWS::RDS::DBCluster`.

2. The rule will then check if that resource has a `DeletionPolicy`.

3. The rule will then check if the `DeletionPolicy` is either `Retain` or `Snapshot`.

4. If the `DeletionPolicy` is **not** set or is set to `Delete`, the rule will return `Warning`.

We will create a directory called `custom_rules` and create a Python file there called `rdsdeletionpolicy.py`.

> **Important note**
>
> In order for `cfn-lint` to process the custom rule properly, you must make sure that your class name and the rule's filename are exactly the same.
>
> This will work: `myrule.py` - `class MyRule(CloudFormationLinterRule)`.
>
> This will not work: `my_rule.py` - `class MyRule(CloudFormationLinterRule)`.

First, we need to come up with a rule number. `cfn-lint` has a list of category rules. The category we can take is `W9001` (W stands for warning, and `9XXX` is reserved for user rules).

Each custom rule is a Python class that inherits from the `CloudFormationLintRule` class. Since this class object belongs to the `cfnlint` Python module, we need to install it using `pip` and, in order to not mess up our system libraries, we will create a Python virtual environment, `Virtualenv`:

```
$ pip install virtualenv
$ virtualenv venv
$ source venv/bin/activate
(venv)$ pip install cfnlint
```

We start with importing the required modules and creating our rule class skeleton:

rdsdeletionpolicy.py

```
from cfnlint.rules import CloudFormationLintRule
from cfnlint.rules import RuleMatch


class RdsDeletionPolicy(CloudFormationLintRule):
    """This rule is used to verify if resources
AWS::RDS::DBInstance
    and AWS::RDS::DBCluster have a deletion policy set to
Snapshot or Retain"""
    id = 'W9001'
    shortdesc = 'Check RDS deletion policy'
    description = 'This rule checks DeletionPolicy on RDS
resources to be Snapshot or Retain'


    def match(self, cfn):
        matches = []
        # Your Rule code goes here
        return matches
```

We have initialized an empty array called `matches`. This array will contain resources that match our rule.

Now we need to parse the template, obtain only RDS resources we want to evaluate, and check if they have a `DeletionPolicy`. We need to add the code to the `match` function:

rdsdeletionpolicy.py (partial)

```
    def match(self, cfn):
        matches = []
        resources = cfn.get_resources(["AWS::RDS::DBInstance",
"AWS::RDS::DBCluster"])
        for resource_name, resource in resources.items():
            deletion_policy = resource.get("DeletionPolicy")
            path = ['Resources', resource_name]
            if not deletion_policy:
```

```
            message = f"Resource {resource_name} does not
have Deletion Policy!"
            matches.append(RuleMatch(path, message))
          elif deletion_policy not in ["Snapshot", "Retain"]:
            message = f"Resource {resource_name} does not
have Deletion Policy set to Snapshot or Retain!"
            matches.append(RuleMatch(path, message))
    return matches
```

Now let's see what our rule looks like:

rdsdeletionpolicy.py

```python
from cfnlint import CloudFormationLintRule
from cfnlint import RuleMatch


class RdsDeletionPolicy(CloudFormationLintRule):
    # ...

    def match(self, cfn):
        matches = []
        resources = cfn.get_resources(["AWS::RDS::DBInstance",
"AWS::RDS::DBCluster"])
        for resource_name, resource in resources.items():
            deletion_policy = resource.get("DeletionPolicy")
            path = ['Resources', resource_name]
            if not deletion_policy:
                message = f"Resource {resource_name} does not
have Deletion Policy!"
                matches.append(RuleMatch(path, message))
            elif deletion_policy not in ["Snapshot", "Retain"]:
                message = f"Resource {resource_name} does not
have Deletion Policy set to Snapshot or Retain!"
                matches.append(RuleMatch(path, message))
        return matches
```

As you can see, we are performing the actions explained previously (in the linter rule workflow). We obtain all the DB resources, and we check whether each of them has a proper Deletion Policy.

Now we can check this linter rule! This is an example that shows how we can check our template's compliance with our own rules:

```
(venv)$ deactivate
$ cfn-lint database_failing.yaml -a custom_rules
W9001 Resource TestDatabase does not have Deletion Policy!
database_failing.yaml:42:3

W9001 Resource ProdDatabase does not have Deletion Policy set
to Snapshot or Retain!
database_failing.yaml:65:3
```

`cfn-lint` and template validation are important parts of the stack deployment process. We will return to them in the next chapter, when we discuss continuous delivery. But before that, let's look at how to provision our resources.

Provisioning our stack

In the first chapter, we created our stack with a simple command:

```
$ aws cloudformation create-stack --stack-name ... --template-body file://...
```

This command invokes a CloudFormation API, `CreateStack`. CloudFormation's API receives the template and parameters in the request body and starts the creation of the stack.

When we want to update our stack (for example, make changes to the existing resources or add new ones), we invoke another API, `UpdateStack`:

```
$ aws cloudformation update-stack --stack-name ... --template-body file://...
```

In both cases, AWS CLI will invoke the `ListStacks` API method in order to check whether the stack exists or not.

If the stack exists during the creation operation, you will receive an error:

```
An error occurred (AlreadyExistsException) when calling the
CreateStack operation: Stack [...] already exists
```

If you try to update a stack that does not exist, you will receive another error:

```
An error occurred (ValidationError) when calling the
UpdateStack operation: Stack [foo] does not exist
```

Note that this is a `ValidationError`. As you may remember, before resources begin to be provisioned, CloudFormation always validates the template to check that the template can be used.

A long time ago, when CloudFormation only supported templates in YAML format, the `CreateStack` and `UpdateStack` API methods were the only way to provision and update resources. There were (and still are) several issues with using these methods. First, it is hard to integrate `create-stack` and `update-stack` subcommands in CI/CD pipelines when we want to make them universal and reusable pipelines templates, because we don't know if we are provisioning a new stack or updating an existing one. We have to use a workaround by executing the `list-stacks` subcommand in order to check whether the stack exists and then decide which operation to run. Another workaround is to create stacks manually first and only use `update-stack` in the CI/CD pipeline, but then we would lose our developer's autonomy.

Second, when we update the stack this way, we might have a lot of changes and it is hard to predict what changes will apply or whether these changes will destroy important resources. We have to either make small or even granular changes or spend a lot of time on code review, thus reducing the speed of development.

In order to solve this problem, the CloudFormation development team has introduced a feature called **Change Sets**.

Deploying stacks using Change Sets

Change Sets (as the name suggests) are the set of changes that will be applied to the stack during the deployment.

We can create, review, execute, or even delete Change Sets, depending on whether the changes that will be applied are desirable.

For this example, we will deploy part of our core template, create a change set for this stack (including additional resources), then review and execute it:

```
$ aws cloudformation create-stack \
                    --stack-name core \
                    --template-body file://core_partial.yaml\
                    --parameters-file file://testing.json
```

When the stack is created, we can examine the **Change Sets** tab and verify that it is empty:

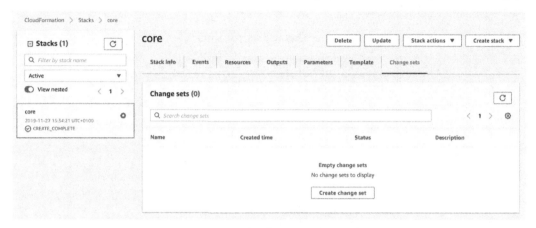

Figure 3.1 – CloudFormation console

Let's create a Change Set:

```
$ aws cloudformation create-change-set \
                    --stack-name core \
                    --change-set-name our-change-set \
                    --template-body file://core_full.yaml \
                    --parameters file://testing.json \
                    --capabilities CAPABILITY_IAM
```

We will receive the following output (yours will differ):

```
{
    "Id": "arn:aws:cloudformation:REGION:ACCT_ID:changeSet/
our-change-set/bd04aeb3-386b-44d7-a25c-5fe626c24aed",
    "StackId": "arn:aws:cloudformation:REGION:ACCT_ID:stack/
core/00697420-1123-11ea-9d40-02433c861a1c"
}
```

We can review this Change Set either in AWS Console or in AWS CLI.

Via AWS CLI, it will look like the following (again, yours might differ because of the different AWS account and/or AWS region):

```
$ aws cloudformation describe-change-set \
                    --change-set-name
arn:aws:cloudformation:REGION:ACCT_ID:changeSet/our-change-set/
bd04aeb3-386b-44d7-a25c-5fe626c24aed
```

The output will be long because there are many changes, so I will only include part of it:

```
{
    "Changes": [
        {
            "Type": "Resource",
            "ResourceChange": {
                "Action": "Add",
                "LogicalResourceId": "AdminRole",
                "ResourceType": "AWS::IAM::Role",
                "Scope": [],
                "Details": []
            }
        },
        {
            "Type": "Resource",
            "ResourceChange": {
                "Action": "Add",
                "LogicalResourceId": "DevRole",
                "ResourceType": "AWS::IAM::Role",
                "Scope": [],
                "Details": []
            }
        },
# The rest of the output...
}
```

In the lower half, we have the metadata of the Change Set, but for now we're interested in this bit:

```
{
        "Type": "Resource",
        "ResourceChange": {
            "Action": "Add",
            "LogicalResourceId": "AdminRole",
            "ResourceType": "AWS::IAM::Role",
            "Scope": [],
            "Details": []
}
}
```

Since we added a new resource, the Action in this Change Set is set to Add. If we remove the resource from the template, we would see Remove, and if the resource had been changed in the template we'd see Modify.

Let's examine this Change Set in the AWS Console:

Figure 3.2 – CloudFormation console – Change Sets tab

When we click on **our-change-set**, we will see its internals:

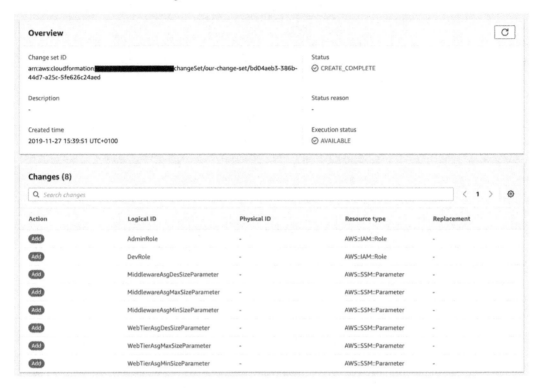

Figure 3.3 – CloudFormation console – our-change-set review

All in all, the outcome is the same, but is more human-friendly to review.

Once we've reviewed the changes, we can deploy this Change Set:

```
$ aws cloudformation execute-change-set --change-set-name
our-change-set --stack-name core
```

Last but not least, another useful subcommand called deploy is used like this:

```
$ aws cloudformation deploy --stack-name foo --template-file
bar
```

The difference between deploy and create-stack or update-stack is that this command is immutable. If you run deploy on the new stack, CloudFormation will create it. If the stack already exists, CloudFormation will update it.

The main differences are as follows:

- `deploy` runs stack provisioning using Change Sets.

- `deploy` uses the `--template-file` argument instead of `--template-body`.

- `deploy` doesn't support parameter files. Instead, you have to specify parameters in the `--parameter-overrides` argument.

- `deploy` will not just return `stackId` in response, but it will wait until the stack is created or fails (which comes in handy when we include CloudFormation commands in the CI/CD pipeline).

To provision the core stack using `deploy`, we need to run the following command:

```
$ aws cloudformation deploy \
                    --stack-name core \
                    --template-file core_full.yaml \
                    --capabilities CAPABILITY_IAM \
                    --parameter-overrides \
                    VpcCidr="10.1.0.0/16" \
                    Environment="test"
```

Since the `deploy` subcommand is the easiest and most redundant way to provision stacks and resources, we will stick to it in the upcoming chapters.

Handling errors

The default and the only behavior of CloudFormation stack deployment in response to errors is to roll back to the previous state.

While this is the proper way to manage a production infrastructure, it might introduce various issues. For example, if you create resources with termination protection and the creation of those resource fails, CloudFormation won't be able to clean up.

For example, we create the WebTier stack, setting `DeletionProtection` to `True` on the `LoadBalancer`.

This is what our load balancer resource looks like:

webtier_failing.yaml

```yaml
WebTierLoadBalancer:
  Type: "AWS::ElasticLoadBalancingV2::LoadBalancer"
  Properties:
    Type: application
    LoadBalancerAttributes:
      - Key: "deletion_protection.enabled"
        Value: True
  # the rest of properties...
```

At the same time, we have a `WebInstance` security group that has a mistake. It will fail to create and therefore triggers the rollback:

webtier_failing.yaml

```yaml
WebInstanceSg:
  Type: "AWS::EC2::SecurityGroup"
  DependsOn: WebTierLoadBalancer
  Properties:
    GroupDescription: WebTier Instance SG
    SecurityGroupIngress:
      - IpProtocol: notexist # will fail
        SourceSecurityGroupId: !Ref WebTierLbSg
        FromPort: 80
        ToPort: 80
  # the rest of the properties...
```

What we will see in the output of the `aws cloudformation deploy` command is that the stack failed to be created. But in the console, we will see a really unpleasant error message:

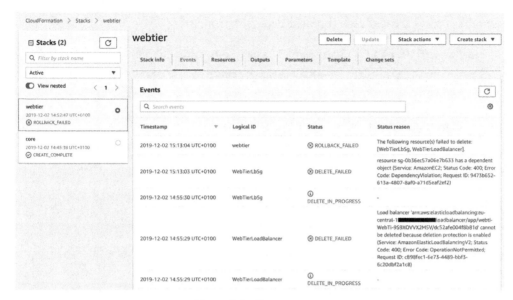

Figure 3.4 – Error message

CloudFormation has to delete the stack, but at the same time the resource is protected from termination. If we hit the **Delete** button in the console, we will see the same error.

We are stuck now. We can't reupdate the stack and we can't delete the stack at the same time! To get rid of this situation, all we have to do is to remove termination protection from the balancer manually and delete the stack again. Another option is to retain those resources, but we are unlikely to want to do that when the initial stack creation fails.

Working with drifts

We covered drifts in the first chapter, *CloudFormation Refresher*. A **drift** is a change in a CloudFormation resource that was not applied by CloudFormation. Although most drifts are created by changes made in the AWS Console or API, some drifts appear even if we provision resources with CloudFormation.

Let's look at the example in the core stack. First, we need to deploy the stack:

```
$ aws cloudformation deploy \
            --template-file core_full.yaml \
            --stack-name core \
            --parameter-overrides \
            VpcCidr=10.1.0.0/16 \
            Environment=test \
            --capabilities CAPABILITY_IAM
```

When the stack is created, let's run drift detection from `awscli`:

```
$ aws cloudformation detect-stack-resource-drift \
                    --stack-name core \
                    --logical-resource-id DevRole
```

In the long output, we will see an interesting change:

```
{
    "StackResourceDrift": {
        "StackId": "arn:aws:cloudformation:REGION:ACCT_
ID:stack/core/32861920-16a7-11ea-bd3e-064a8d32fc9e",
        "LogicalResourceId": "DevRole",
        "PhysicalResourceId": "core-DevRole-G5L6EMSFH153",
        "ResourceType": "AWS::IAM::Role",
        "ExpectedProperties": ...,
        "ActualProperties": ...,
        "PropertyDifferences": [
            {
                "PropertyPath": "/AssumeRolePolicyDocument/
Statement/0/Principal/AWS",
                "ExpectedValue": "ACCT_ID",
                "ActualValue": "arn:aws:iam::ACCT_ID:root",
                "DifferenceType": "NOT_EQUAL"
            }
        ],
        "StackResourceDriftStatus": "MODIFIED",
        "Timestamp": "..."
    }
}
```

So, what happened? When we set the `Principal` for the IAM role to `DevRole`, we set its `Principal` attribute the value of `!Ref "AWS::AccountId"`. But when the stack is created, CloudFormation (or IAM) rewrites it to the full path to the root user (which is essentially the same as storing the AWS account ID).

Although that doesn't introduce many issues, we want to keep our stack drift clean. So, in this case, the only thing we can do is to set the right `Principal` value so it doesn't get rewritten.

Another situation is when there is an unmanaged change. Let's add an additional policy to our IAM role:

```
$ aws iam attach-role-policy \
        --role-name core-DevRole-G5L6EMSFH153 \
        --policy-arn \
        arn:aws:iam::aws:policy/AmazonEC2FullAccess
```

For ease of understanding, run drift detection from the console:

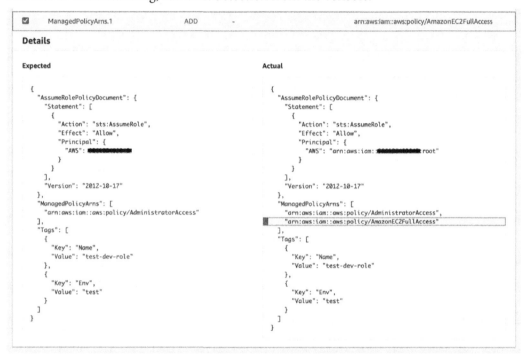

Figure 3.5 – CloudFormation console

What we can do is remove that policy manually. But if for some reason we can't do that (let's say we have no access to the API), then we can make this change by adding this policy in the template and executing the deployment again:

core_drift.yaml

```
DevRole:
    Type: "AWS::IAM::Role"
    Properties:
        # some properties...
```

```
      ManagedPolicyArns:
          - !If [ ProdEnv, "arn:aws:iam::aws:policy/
ReadOnlyAccess", "arn:aws:iam::aws:policy/AdministratorAccess"]
          - "arn:aws:iam::aws:policy/AmazonEC2FullAccess"
```

We update the stack one more time:

```
$ aws cloudformation deploy \
                    --template-file core_drift.yaml \
                    --stack-name core \
                    --parameter-overrides \
                    VpcCidr=10.1.0.0/16 \
                    Environment=test \
                    --capabilities CAPABILITY_IAM
```

And we can see that this drift is gone:

Figure 3.6 – The drift is gone

If this is an undesired change, all we have to do is to delete the policy from the role in the template, and it will be removed in IAM.

We were able to resolve this drift by adding the policy to the CloudFormation template.

> **Important note**
>
> At the time of writing, the AWS CloudFormation team has released a new feature called Resource Import, which allows you to add existing resources to your stack.
>
> This is a long-awaited functionality that helps us to migrate to Infrastructure-as-Code practices with few issues, but it is as yet impossible to import drifts into the CloudFormation stack. But stay tuned!

Drift management is a complex task. As AWS engineers, we want to expect that CloudFormation developers will add more features, but it is our job to make sure that all the changes in the infrastructure are done only via CloudFormation.

Summary

In this chapter, we've covered various ways of provisioning a stack.

We've learned how to make sure that our stack will not fail to deploy, and our resources will provision as we want. We've also written our very first (but definitely not our last) linter rule, making our infrastructure code more reliable and our development process more efficient.

We've learned about Change Sets and how they advance the manner of stack deployments. We now know how to handle errors and how we can import the changes manually.

In the next chapter, we will recycle our knowledge and apply automation to CloudFormation using AWS development services such as `CodeCommit`, `CodeBuild`, and `CodePipeline`.

Questions

1. Which category in `cfn-lint` is reserved for custom rules?
2. What is the difference between template linting and validation?
3. What happens when you run `aws cloudformation deploy ...`?
4. Can you have two different Change Sets with the same name?
5. What are the requirements for naming customer rules in `cfn-lint`?
6. How can you move the detected drift in the stack if the unmanaged change is desirable?

Further reading

- CloudFormation linter: `https://github.com/aws-cloudformation/cfn-python-lint`

- Importing resources in the stack: `https://docs.aws.amazon.com/AWSCloudFormation/latest/UserGuide/resource-import.html`

- Working with drifts: `https://docs.aws.amazon.com/AWSCloudFormation/latest/UserGuide/using-cfn-stack-drift.html`

4
Continuous Integration and Deployment

We know how to build our templates, and we know how to make sure they are valid and how to deploy them. Now it is time to apply another block of DevOps, called **Continuous Delivery (CD)**. CD is used to test our applications against real-life scenarios and deploy them seamlessly so that the end user notices the changes once they refresh the page. This means no downtime and no *The page is under maintenance* messages.

In **Infrastructure as Code (IaC)**, you treat your infrastructure and resources as a computer application. Although you cannot perform unit tests against your templates, you still have various options for how to run a proper Continuous Delivery pipeline.

In this chapter, we will learn how to include our templates in our applications. We will also learn how we can test our stacks and how we can apply **Amazon Web Services CloudFormation (AWS CloudFormation)** in Continuous Delivery practices. By the end of this chapter, we will be able to apply a CI/CD pipeline with CloudFormation.

We will look at the following:

- Including a template in your application
- Running smoke tests on your stack
- Best practices for the release management of CloudFormation stacks
- Creating a CI/CD pipeline with CloudFormation and CodePipeline

Technical requirements

The code used in this chapter can be found in the book's GitHub repository at `https://github.com/PacktPublishing/Mastering-AWS-CloudFormation/tree/master/Chapter4`.

Check out the following video to see the Code in Action:

`https://bit.ly/2yWmAox`

Including a template in your application

You will recall from the previous chapters that we had several templates for different tiers. We had *core* (network and security), *web* (frontend), *middleware* (backend), and *database* tiers.

So far, we haven't stored our templates in the version control system, but since we need to apply Continuous Delivery, we need to figure out the proper way to store them. Normally, it all depends on how you want to organize your workflow. If you have a separate operations or *cloud* team that is responsible for infrastructure and operations, it is wise to keep all the templates in a single repository. Developers will then supply you with any desired changes to the infrastructure or with the new version of the application.

Our flow is as follows:

1. The developer publishes a new version of an app.
2. The developer provides the operations team with the new version and/or changes.
3. The operations team makes changes to parameters and/or templates.
4. The operations team deploys the changes to the stack.

Although this sounds logical, just think about how this flow would work in the real world. It could take several hours—or even days—until the new version went into production! DevOps culture is all about collaboration between developers and operations, which is why it is wise to mix the flow and let both parties take responsibility for the infrastructure.

So, it is wise to *include* the template in the application repository. Look at the template as the configuration of your application. We know what our application needs to have in order to run, so why not include it?

The repository for this kind of application, including the app, and including the configuration files, would look like the following:

```
my_app/
|----.git/
|----config
|    |----test
|    |    |----config.ini
|    |----prod
|         |----config.ini
|----src/
|    |---- # your source code here
|----tests/
|    |---- # your tests here
|----cloudformation/
     |----template.yaml
```

This would require your developers to learn how to use AWS CloudFormation, but their hard work will definitely pay off.

For some resources, this method will not work. For example, Core stack is not a part of any application, so we will have to keep it in a separate repository.

In this chapter, we will cover both scenarios. But before we build our first pipeline, we need to understand what the steps for it are and how we can understand whether our infrastructure is deployed and operating as expected.

Running smoke tests on your stack

How do we know whether our application is healthy once it is deployed?

In addition to monitoring, logging, and alerting, there is a method called **smoke testing**.

Smoke testing is a method of testing that is applied during or after an application's release. It helps us to understand whether the current release is functional or whether it contains several bugs or failures that require immediate rollback.

CloudFormation has an out-of-the-box rollback feature. As we know, it will roll back our stack to the previous `healthy` state if at least one of the changes could not be applied or a resource cannot be created. From the perspective of AWS, it is usually an AWS service that reports that the resource creation has failed and that the error we are seeing is actually an error message from AWS' API. However, some resources are not reported on if they have failed to create by design.

Smoke testing for EC2 auto scaling groups

For example, we provision an **autoscaling group (ASG)** with an **Elastic Load Balancer (ELB)**. An ASG will run one or more instances from either the launch configuration or the launch template. The launch configuration might have a set of commands to run during the creation of an **EC2** instance. We can install web server software on an instance while provisioning and set the ASG to replace an instance if the ELB health checks fail on it. We can provision all of this with CloudFormation.

The following is an example template (part of the resources is missing because I'm using a *default VPC*). For the full template, look in the following source code:

broken_asg.yaml (partial)

```yaml
AWSTemplateFormatVersion: "2010-09-09"
Parameters:
  # ...
Resources:
  Lc:
    Type: AWS::AutoScaling::LaunchConfiguration
    Properties:
      ImageId: !Ref AmiId
      InstanceType: t2.micro
      UserData: # can you find a mistake in this UserData?
        Fn::Base64: |
          #!/bin/bash
          yum -y install yolo
          systemctl start yolo
      SecurityGroups:
        - !Ref Sg
  Asg:
    Type: AWS::AutoScaling::AutoScalingGroup
```

```
    Properties:
        # ...
        LaunchConfigurationName: !Ref Lc
        # ...
# The rest of the resources...
Outputs:
    Dns:
        Value: !GetAtt Elb.DNSName
```

When we deploy this template, CloudFormation will report that the creation of the stack is complete:

```
$ aws cloudformation deploy \
                --template-file broken_asg.yaml \
                --stack-name broken \
                --parameter-overrides VpcId=vpc-12345678\
                SubnetIds=subnet-123,subnet-456,subnet-
789,subnet-012,subnet-345,subnet-678
Waiting for changeset to be created..
Waiting for stack create/update to complete
Successfully created/updated stack - broken
```

However, if we try to go via the URL of the ELB from the CloudFormation output, we will see the following:

```
$ aws cloudformation describe-stacks --stack-name broken | jq
.[][].Outputs[].OutputValue
"broken-Elb-157OHF7S5UYIC-1875871321.us-east-1.elb.amazonaws.
com"
$ curl broken-Elb-157OHF7S5UYIC-1875871321.us-east-1.elb.
amazonaws.com
<html>
<head><title>503 Service Temporarily Unavailable</title></head>
<body bgcolor="white">
<center><h1>503 Service Temporarily Unavailable</h1></center>
</body>
</html>
```

Why does this happen? If the stack is created, that means the infrastructure is in place and everything *should* be fine. However, if we open the EC2 console, we can see that the instances are being terminated one by one:

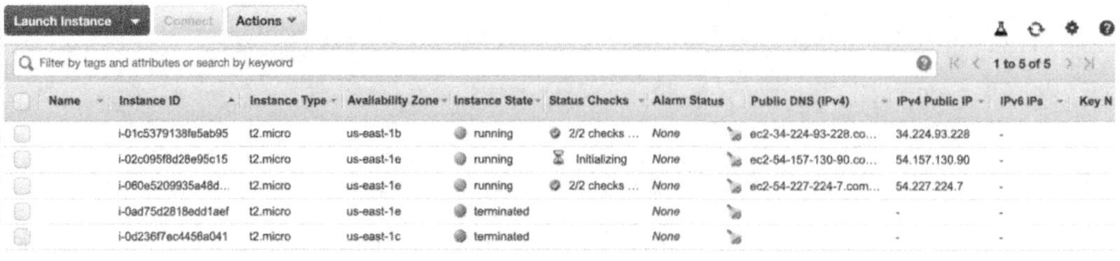

Figure 4.1 – The AWS EC2 console

This occurs because the launch configuration's *user data* is malfunctioning (as you may have noticed, I haven't installed any web server software). An ASG has also been created and the instances are being launched and terminated, but CloudFormation is not aware of that; it received the API response from EC2 and the ASG.

There is an easy way to solve this problem using ASGs (we will look into this in *Chapter 6, Configuration Management of the EC2 Instances Using cfn-init*), but for now, just keep in mind that these kinds of issues might occur and CloudFormation cannot deal with them out of the box.

Another problem with testing our templates is that CloudFormation doesn't have any unit testing abilities, such as common programming languages. The only way to test them is to provision the stack from the template and run tests against the stack and its resources.

There are several ways of checking application stacks, but the simplest is to make an HTTP request to a health check endpoint (in our case, /).

Our test suite will be a small Python script, which will do the following:

1. Parse the argument (the stack name).

2. Make a request to the CloudFormation API to get the stack output (the ELB DNS name).

3. Make an HTTP request to that DNS name.

4. If the script doesn't receive a 200 OK HTTP response, it will print Stack deployment failed! and exit with code 1.

This is how our testing script will look:

asg_test.py

```python
# imports ...
try:
    stack = sys.argv[1]
except IndexError:
    print("Please provide a stack name")
    sys.exit(1)
cfn_client = boto3.client('cloudformation')
try:
    stack = cfn_client.describe_stacks(StackName=stack)
except botocore.exceptions.ClientError:
    print("This stack does not exist or region is incorrect")
    sys.exit(1)
elb_dns = stack['Stacks'][0]['Outputs'][0]['OutputValue']
for _ in range(0, 2):
    resp = requests.get(f"http://{elb_dns}")
    if resp.status_code == 200:
        print("Test succeeded")
        sys.exit(0)
    sleep(5)
print(f"Result of test: {resp.content}")
print(f"HTTP Response code: {resp.status_code}")
print("Test did not succeed")
sys.exit(1)
```

If we run it against our stack again, we will get the following result:

```
$ python asg_test.py broken
Result of test: b'<html>\r\n<head><title>503 Service
Temporarily Unavailable</title></head>\r\n<body
bgcolor="white">\r\n<center><h1>503 Service Temporarily
Unavailable</h1></center>\r\n</body>\r\n</html>\r\n'
HTTP Response code: 503
Test did not succeed
```

Now, we have to figure out what went wrong with the template. Once we find a problem (which, in this case, is in the launch configuration's *user data*), we can fix it and rerun the stack deployment and test our resources again:

working_asg.yaml

```yaml
# Parameters section...
Resources:
  Lc:
    Type: AWS::AutoScaling::LaunchConfiguration
    Properties:
      ImageId: !Ref AmiId
      InstanceType: t2.micro
      UserData:
        Fn::Base64: |
          #!/bin/bash
          amazon-linux-extras install -y epel
          yum -y install nginx
          systemctl start nginx
      SecurityGroups:
        - !Ref Sg
# the rest of the template...
```

Once the working template is deployed, we can run our script again:

```
$ python asg_test.py broken
Test succeeded
```

While this is just an example of this case, we know that we cannot use this test suite for other stacks and resources. Depending on what we are building, we must create a new test case for every application or infrastructure that we deploy.

For services, such as VPC networks, **IAM** roles, and DynamoDB tables, CloudFormation can ensure that resources are properly configured. But how do we know that they are doing what they are supposed to do?

Smoke testing VPC resources

Let's look again at our *core* template. We know it has *private* and *public* subnets. Let's say we want to check whether subnets that are supposed to be private are associated with a private route table (the one that routes traffic through a NAT gateway).

To carry out this test, we need to do the following:

1. First, append your subnet resources with an extra tag.

    Use the following tag for public subnets:

    ```
    - Key: 'Private'
      Value: 'False'
    ```

    Use the following tag for private subnets:

    ```
    - Key: 'Private'
      Value: 'True'
    ```

2. Our script will gather the stack's resources, not its outputs. Filter the resources to be of the `AWS::EC2::Subnet` type and make the value of the `Private` tag `"True"`.

3. Obtain the ID of the private route table and then check whether private subnets are associated with the private Route Table ID.

4. The following steps will give us a test suite for the VPC subnets:

5. First, parse the arguments and verify that the stack exists:

core_subnets.py

```python
# imports...
matches = []
try:
    stack = sys.argv[1]
except IndexError:
    print("Please provide a stack name")
    sys.exit(1)
cfn_client = boto3.client('cloudformation')
try:
```

```
        resources = cfn_client.describe_stack_
resources(StackName=stack)
```

```
except botocore.exceptions.ClientError:
```

```
        print("This stack does not exist or region is
incorrect")
```

```
        sys.exit(1)
```

6.   Then, obtain the ID of the private route table and all of the subnets in the stack:

core_subnets.py

```
subnets_in_stack = []
```

```
for resource in resources['StackResources']:
```

```
        if resource['LogicalResourceId'] ==
"PrivateRouteTable":
```

```
            private_route_table =
resource['PhysicalResourceId']
```

```
        if resource['ResourceType'] == "AWS::EC2::Subnet":
subnets_in_stack.append(resource['PhysicalResourceId'])
```

7.   Finally, obtain the subnets' association using the EC2 API, match their tags, and
     check that they have the necessary route table association:

core_subnets.py

```
ec2_client = boto3.client('ec2')
```

```
subnets_to_check = []
```

```
for subnet in subnets_in_stack:
```

```
        resp = ec2_client.describe_subnets(SubnetIds=[subnet])
```

```
        for tag in resp['Subnets'][0]['Tags']:
```

```
            if tag['Key'] == "Private" and tag['Value'] ==
"True":
```

```
                subnets_to_check.append(subnet)
```

```
route_table = ec2_client.describe_route_
tables(RouteTableIds=[private_route_table])
```

```
private_subnets = []
```

```
for assoc in route_table['RouteTables'][0]
['Associations']:
```

```
        private_subnets.append(assoc['SubnetId'])
for subnet in subnets_to_check:
    if subnet not in private_subnets:
        matches.append(subnet)
if matches:
    print("One or more private subnets are not associated
with proper route table!")
    print(f"Non-compliant subnets: {matches}")
    sys.exit(1)
print("All subnets are compliant!")
exit(0)
```

8. Let's deploy our stack and try this test case:

```
$ aws cloudformation deploy --stack-name core --template-
file core_non_compliant.yaml --capabilities CAPABILITY_
IAM

Waiting for changeset to be created..
Waiting for stack create/update to complete
Successfully created/updated stack - core
$ python core_subnets.py core
One or more private subnets are not associated with
proper route table!
Non-compliant subnets: ['subnet-0b087c910c675cd5d',
'subnet-037acf2fce30c38fd', 'subnet-041e96329b5d1449a']
```

We've received an error, which means our core stack has non-compliant subnets! Let's now deploy a stack with proper association and try this test again:

```
$ aws cloudformation deploy --stack-name core --template-
file core_compliant.yaml --capabilities CAPABILITY_IAM

Waiting for changeset to be created..
Waiting for stack create/update to complete
Successfully created/updated stack - core
$ python core_subnets.py core
All subnets are compliant!
```

Again, this is just an example of a particular case. Depending on how you organize your CloudFormation templates, you will figure out how to carry out proper testing.

> **Important note**
>
> Do we really need to perform these actions during stack operations? Try to work out how you can avoid carrying out these tests once the stack is deployed. By the end, we are making sure that the resources have proper attributes and/or associations. Think about how you can come to a solution by using `cfn-lint`.

We now know how to perform testing on a template, so let's move on to the next topic.

Best practices for the release management of CloudFormation stacks

Before we build our very first pipeline for Continuous Delivery, I want to focus on this important topic. In this section, we will go through the best practices for the release management of CloudFormation stacks.

By the end, we want to treat our infrastructure like a computer program, so let's use the experience of software development!

Always use version control systems

Your infrastructure is now code. So, you need to have version control on it. **Version control systems** (**VCS**) have several benefits, including code collaboration, change history, centralized storage for source code, integration with build systems, and much more.

In order to keep your infrastructure clean and well-maintained and your changes well-observed, always keep your CloudFormation templates in VCS.

Ensuring that your dependencies can be easily retrieved

In this and the previous chapter, we developed several scripts for our templates, including custom linter rules and smoke tests.

These scripts have external dependencies (`pip` packages, in our case), so you want to make sure that they can be installed and resolved easily.

Keeping your code base clean

Make sure you properly organize your CloudFormation repository. Store smoke tests in the tests folder, parameters where they should be, and custom linter rules in a proper directory (such as custom_rules). If you store your template with a *monorepo* model, create a subdirectory for each group or project so they can be easily maintained.

Choosing a proper branching model

In most software projects, the *master* branch is considered to be a production branch. It is important to choose your branching model wisely so that you can integrate your source code with the CI/CD systems.

You can break up your workflow in the dev/test/master branches so that the CI/CD system runs specific stages on specific branches. You don't need to deploy each commit to the production stack, so for the dev branch, you are likely to only do validation and linting.

If you use project management tools, such as **Jira**, make sure that you add the issue key to a commit message:

```
git commit -m "PROJ-1234 add extra subnets for databases"
```

Making clear comments and including project or issue keys will help you to keep the code base clean and the development process transparent.

Always perform a code review

Do not allow a direct push to master and use pull requests to control upcoming changes. Even if the linter is happy and all the tests pass, there may be a case where a faulty configuration gets into the production stack. Even if CloudFormation is able to roll back, it is always wise to prevent this from happening by reviewing each change.

Having full test coverage

It is important that you always perform linting and template validation before deploying changes to the stack. You cannot perform unit testing against CloudFormation templates, but you still need to ensure that as few errors are reaching CloudFormation as possible. Focus on developing custom rules for cfn-lint so that you can implement best practices for your organization.

Don't forget to use a CloudFormation IAM role

As you will remember, when we deploy a stack, we use our own IAM privileges. This means that we must have at least an administrator access policy on AWS, which is not secure. In addition, since we expect more people to collaborate on the infrastructure, we need to use a CloudFormation IAM role so that we don't provide each template developer with administrator access to AWS.

Always perform smoke testing

If we manage critical infrastructure, we need to ensure that every change is not going to cause a failure or misconfiguration. Deploying a temporary stack with the latest changes in a separate environment (or even separate AWS accounts) and running smoke tests against our stack, combined with proper linting and validation, is best practice to prevent mistakes.

Using the correct CI/CD instruments

Stack operations (validation, linting, and deployment) are basic commands. However, we need to be sure that CI/CD systems can perform them. We need to choose functionality and costs wisely. Moreover, we need to think about security because we are providing access to our AWS account. If we have strict security requirements, we'll likely want to provision a CI/CD system (such as GitLab or Jenkins) in our AWS environment or use AWS managed services, such as CodeBuild or CodePipeline.

Keeping up the good work

Practices and methodologies are evolving and so are instruments. We want to revise the way we carry out Continuous Delivery and see whether there is any room for improvement. Long story short, there always is.

This said, let's move on to the last section of this chapter and build our own Continuous Delivery pipeline for CloudFormation!

Creating a CI/CD pipeline with CloudFormation and CodePipeline

Before we begin creating the pipeline, let's revise what a CI/CD pipeline actually is. Any CI/CD pipeline (in terms of software development) consists of stages.

Those stages are usually as follows (we will practice all of these steps later):

1. **Pre-build**: Pull the code from source code management and install the dependencies.

2. **Build**: Run the build and retrieve the artifacts.

3. **Test**: Run a test suite against the build.

4. **Package**: Store the build artifacts in the artifact storage.

5. **Deploy**: Deploy a new version on the environment.

If any of these steps fail, the build system will trigger an error.

So, how can we apply the same steps on CloudFormation? Usually, it depends on the **Continuous Integration** (**CI**) system. In our case, these stages will do the following:

- **Pre-build**: Store the code (for example, the templates) in AWS CodeCommit and use AWS CodeBuild as a build system. We will also pull the code from CodeCommit and install the necessary dependency packages, including the following:
- `cfn-lint`
- `awscli`
- `boto3` and `botocore` (an AWS SDK for Python)
- **Build**: This stage will be skipped. Why? Because CloudFormation templates aren't like any software source code. For example, we do not need to compile them. Instead, we can run a validation check:

```
aws cloudformation validate-template --template-body ...
```

At this stage, this will be enough. The reason we don't run validation checks during the test phase is that validation is a simple syntax check that is similar to code compilation in the context of CloudFormation.

- **Test**: In this step, we will run `cfn-lint` against our template. If the linter check doesn't fail, we will deploy the new template to a testing environment, run the smoke test, and then terminate it.
- **Package**: In this step, we want to store the artifact (which, in our case, is a template file) in the artifact storage. Since, as a service, AWS CloudFormation uses the template from S3 (a particular bucket), S3 will act as artifact storage for us.

  Once the testing phase is complete, we will upload the changed (or new) template to the S3 bucket.
- **Deploy**: In this step, we will just run the production deployment using the template that was packaged and stored on S3.

Scenario – core stack

We decided to store the core stack as a separate entity of our AWS environment. For the core stack, our flow will look as follows:

Figure 4.2 – The core CI/CD pipeline workflow

If any of these steps fail, the CI/CD system will fire an error and cancel the build.

To perform this task, we will use CodeCommit (the SCM), CodeBuild (the build system), and CodePipeline (the actual CI/CD "connector" system).

We will have to configure the files. The first one will be `buildspec.yaml`—the build specification file with instruction and build stages (this is similar to `Jenkinsfile` in Jenkins). The second will be CloudFormation, which contains all the building blocks for our pipeline: the source code repository, the build project, and the pipeline.

Let's start with `buildspec.yml`. This is how it is going to look in our case:

buildspec.yml

```
version: 0.2
phases:
  install:
    runtime-versions:
      python: 3.8
```

```
    commands:
      - pip install awscli cfn-lint
  build:
    commands:
      - aws cloudformation validate-template --template-body
file://core.yaml
      - cfn-lint core.yaml
  post_build:
    commands:
      - aws cloudformation deploy --template-file core.yaml
--stack-name core-tmp --capabilities CAPABILITY_NAMED_IAM
--role-arn $CFN_ROLE
      - python tests/core_subnets.py core-tmp
    finally:
      - aws cloudformation delete-stack --stack-name core-tmp
--role-arn $CFN_ROLE
artifacts:
  files:
    - core.yaml
```

We will include this file in the repository, otherwise CodeBuild won't know which actions to perform.

The instructions for CodeBuild are specified in the build specification. The build specification consists of several phases: `install`, `build`, and `post_build`.

During the `install` phase, we install the necessary dependencies, such as `cfn-lint` and `awscli`. During the `build` phase, we run validation and linting. During the `post_build` phase, we run the deployment of a temporary stack, run smoke tests, and delete the stack. If all of the steps are completed successfully, the core template and its parameters are uploaded to S3 (this is defined in the `artifacts` section, but the actual path to S3 is managed in CodePipeline).

If the `post_build` step fails (let's say temporary stack deployment failed or the tests didn't succeed), we stop right there and clean up the temporary stack.

We are going to perform the following actions to get a working CI/CD pipeline:

1. We'll start by looking at our CI/CD template. This template contains the following resources:

   - A repository (CodeCommit)

   - A build project (CodeBuild)

   - Artifacts storage (an S3 bucket)

   - A pipeline (CodePipeline)

   - IAM roles (for CodeBuild, CodePipeline, and, of course, CloudFormation)

2. Let's focus on the important sections of the template. The following code block declares the CodeCommit repository and S3 bucket (which will act as artifact storage for CodePipeline):

cicd.yaml (the SCM repo and artifacts storage)

```
Repository:
  Type: AWS::CodeCommit::Repository
  Properties:
    RepositoryName: core
TemplateBucket:
  Type: AWS::S3::Bucket
```

We don't have to configure much here since the creation of the S3 bucket and CodeCommit repository is a trivial task. However, CodeBuild is a bit more challenging.

3. In the CodeBuild declaration, we need to explicitly declare that the source for the build jobs will be CodePipeline. This instructs CodeBuild to accept API calls from CodePipeline in order to run build jobs:

cicd.yaml (the build project)

```
Build:
  Type: AWS::CodeBuild::Project
```

```
    Properties:
      Artifacts:
        Type: CODEPIPELINE
      ServiceRole: !GetAtt BuildRole.Arn
      Name: Core
      Source:
        Type: CODEPIPELINE
      Environment:
        Type: LINUX_CONTAINER
        ComputeType: BUILD_GENERAL1_SMALL
        Image: aws/codebuild/amazonlinux2-x86_64-
standard:2.0
```

> **Important note**
>
> For `Source` and `Artifacts`, we set the type as CodePipeline. This is
> because the input and the output are supplied to and from CodePipeline, which
> will act as the arbiter and the manager. We don't specify any build steps in the
> template itself. This is because the build steps for CodeBuild are declared in
> `buildspec.yml`.

4. Now, let's investigate what is in our pipeline resource. The pipeline consists of
    three major stages. The first is `Clone`. At this stage, source code is pulled from
    CodeCommit and stored on S3. The S3 object key (for example, the path to the
    code) is also stored as an output artifact:

cicd.yaml (the pipeline)

```
# ...
        - Name: Clone
          Actions:
            - ActionTypeId:
                Category: Source
                Owner: AWS
                Provider: CodeCommit
                Version: "1"
              Name: Clone
```

```
OutputArtifacts:
  - Name: CloneOutput
Configuration:
  BranchName: master
  RepositoryName: !GetAtt Repository.Name
RunOrder: 1
```

5. The second stage is Build. This stage will take the code from S3 (the output artifact from the previous stage) and run the CodeBuild project. If the build's job is successful, the template is also stored on S3 as an output artifact:

cicd.yaml (the pipeline)

```
- Name: Build
  Actions:
    - Name: Build
      InputArtifacts:
        - Name: CloneOutput
      ActionTypeId:
        Category: Build
        Owner: AWS
        Version: "1"
        Provider: CodeBuild
      OutputArtifacts:
        - Name: BuildOutput
      Configuration:
        ProjectName: !Ref Build
      RunOrder: 1
```

6. The last stage is `Deploy`. During this stage, CodePipeline will run stack creation (or update) using the template from the output of the build step:

cicd.yaml (the pipeline)

```
            - Name: Deploy
              Actions:
                - Name: Deploy
                  InputArtifacts:
                    - Name: BuildOutput
                  ActionTypeId:
                    Category: Deploy
                    Owner: AWS
                    Version: "1"
                    Provider: CloudFormation
                  OutputArtifacts:
                    - Name: DeployOutput
                  Configuration:
                    ActionMode: CREATE_UPDATE
                    RoleArn: !GetAtt CfnRole.Arn
                    Capabilities: CAPABILITY_NAMED_IAM
                    StackName: Core
                    TemplatePath: BuildOutput::core.yaml
```

All these stages happen automatically; CodePipeline listens to the repository and launches every time there is a change.

7. Now, let's deploy the CI/CD stack and experiment a bit:

```
aws cloudformation deploy \
            --stack-name cicd \
            --template-file cicd.yaml \
            --capabilities CAPABILITY_IAM
```

Once the stack is deployed, we can add the files one by one. Let's first take a look at our pipeline:

Figure 4.3 – The AWS CodePipeline console

We can already see that it has failed. This is because CodePipeline runs immediately after creation but our repository is empty and there is nothing to pull.

8. Now, let's add the necessary files to the repository. For ease, we'll do it manually, but in production, it will be carried out using `git` commands.

    We need to go to **Source | Repositories | Code**. What we see are instructions on how to clone the repository. We can ignore them for now and click **Add file | Upload file**:

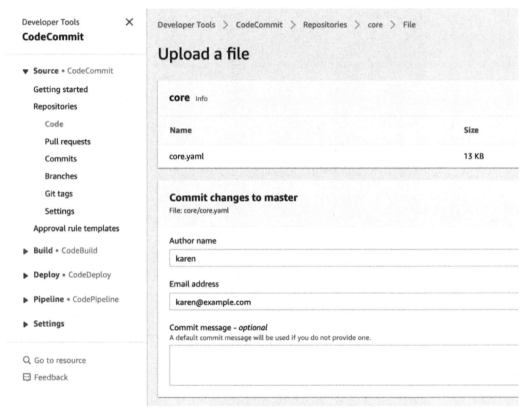

Figure 4.4 – The AWS CodeCommit console

9. We will do the same for the other files we need for the pipeline. By the end, our repository will look like this:

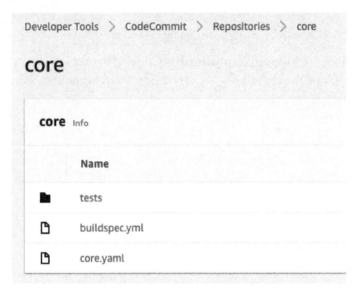

Figure 4.5 – The AWS CodeCommit console

10. Let's go back to CodePipeline:

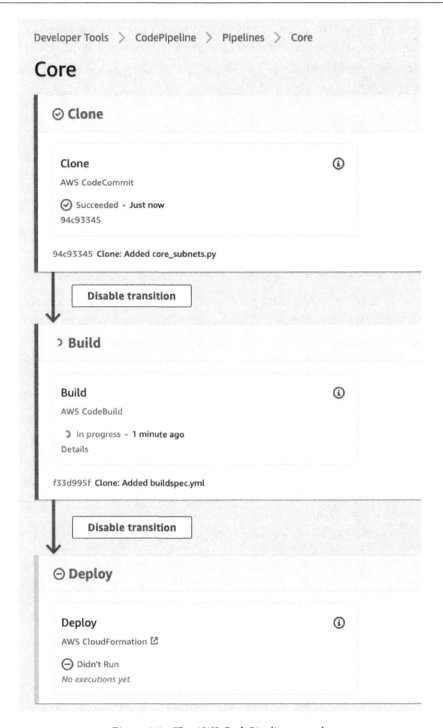

Figure 4.6 – The AWS CodePipeline console

We can already see some action! But unfortunately, these builds are going to fail because the repository isn't complete. Meanwhile, we can look at the build project logs:

```
[Container] 2019/12/19 15:03:19 Running command cfn-lint
core.yaml
[Container] 2019/12/19 15:03:20 Phase complete: BUILD
State: SUCCEEDED
[Container] 2019/12/19 15:03:20 Phase context status
code:  Message:
[Container] 2019/12/19 15:03:21 Entering phase POST_BUILD
[Container] 2019/12/19 15:03:21 Running command aws
cloudformation deploy --template-file core.yaml --stack-
name core-tmp --capabilities CAPABILITY_NAMED_IAM --role-
arn $CFN_ROLE
Waiting for changeset to be created..
Waiting for stack create/update to complete
```

The build system is busy creating the stack. However, it will fail afterward because the test suite was uploaded after `buildspec.yml`. We will see an error such as the following:

```
[Container] 2019/12/19 15:06:18 Running command python
tests/core_subnets.py core-tmp
python: can't open file 'tests/core_subnets.py': [Errno
2] No such file or directory
[Container] 2019/12/19 15:06:18 Command did not exit
successfully python tests/core_subnets.py core-tmp exit
status 2
[Container] 2019/12/19 15:06:18 Running command aws
cloudformation delete-stack --stack-name core-tmp --role-
arn $CFN_ROLE
[Container] 2019/12/19 15:06:19 Phase complete: POST_
BUILD State: FAILED
[Container] 2019/12/19 15:06:19 Phase context status
code: COMMAND_EXECUTION_ERROR Message: Error while
executing command: python tests/core_subnets.py core-tmp.
Reason: exit status 2
```

The next error is as follows (for the pipeline running once we have added the test suite, the error is different):

```
[Container] 2019/12/19 15:06:57 Running command aws
cloudformation deploy --template-file core.yaml --stack-
name core-tmp --capabilities CAPABILITY_NAMED_IAM --role-
arn $CFN_ROLE
```

```
An error occurred (ValidationError) when
calling the CreateChangeSet operation:
Stack:arn:aws:cloudformation:REGIOS:ACCT_ID:stack/core-
tmp/b2960880-2270-11ea-90be-06bc90058f1a is in DELETE_IN_
PROGRESS state and can not be updated.
```

This is because the previous step started deleting the template and the new one tried to deploy the same template. The pipeline now looks really bad:

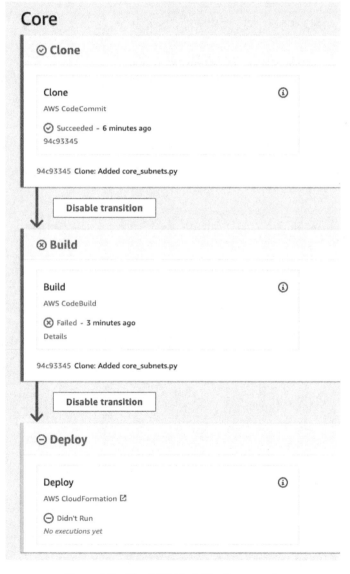

Figure 4.7 – The AWS CodePipeline console

11. However, there is no need to worry! Let's run the whole pipeline again by hitting **Retry** on the **Build** stage. After a while, we can see that the pipeline has succeeded:

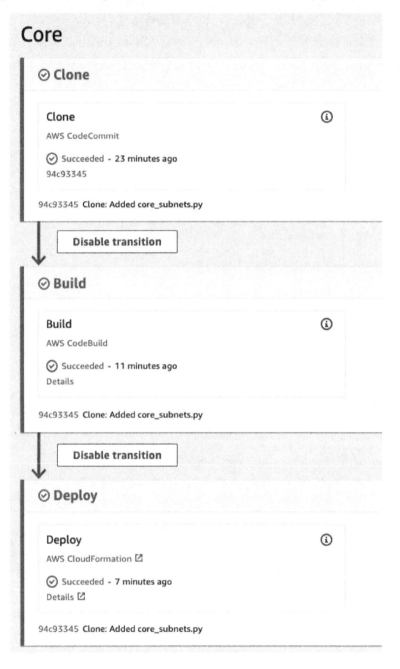

Figure 4.8 – The AWS CodePipeline console

12. We can also see our **Core** stack:

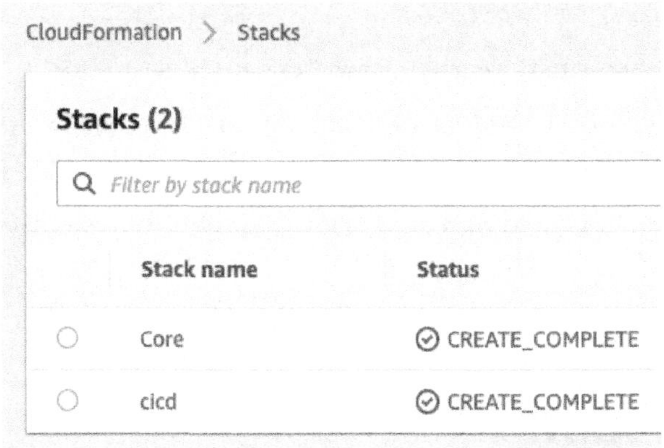

Figure 4.9 – The AWS CloudFormation console

That's it! We now have a fully functional Continuous Delivery pipeline with test coverage!

Summary

In this chapter, we learned how to perform testing against CloudFormation stacks and what the best practices are for Continuous Delivery with CloudFormation.

We also created our very first pipeline using development services in AWS, such as CodeCommit, CodeBuild, and CodePipeline.

Although this pipeline is working and doing what it is supposed to do, there is always room for improvement. Ask yourself what you could add to the pipeline or change to make it more effective.

We should move the creation of the temporary stack from CodeBuild to CodePipeline as an extra stage so we can save some money since, in CodeBuild, you pay for build execution time. Simply put, while CodeBuild waits until the temporary stack has been created, the build job is being billed.

Another thing is that by using the same temporary stack name (`core-tmp`), we are not able to run multiple builds at the same time. If another build runs while `core-tmp` is being deleted by a previous build, we will receive an error.

As mentioned in the *Best practices for the release management of CloudFormation stacks* section, there is always room for improvement.

In the next chapter, we will cover another important topic: *StackSets*. We will learn how to deploy the same stacks in different regions and even accounts!

Questions

1. What is `buildspec.yml`?

2. What are CloudFormation artifacts? Where are they stored?

3. How can you inform CloudFormation about instances where ASGs are not properly provisioned?

4. How can a CloudFormation API provide a list of resources that are provisioned within a stack?

5. What are the building blocks of CodePipeline? Which AWS services are used?

Further reading

- Continuous Delivery with CodePipeline: `https://docs.aws.amazon.com/AWSCloudFormation/latest/UserGuide/continuous-delivery-codepipeline.html`

- Infrastructure Continuous Delivery Using AWS CloudFormation: `https://www.slideshare.net/AmazonWebServices/infrastructure-continuous-delivery-using-aws-cloudformation-73808130`

5

Deploying to Multiple Regions and Accounts Using StackSets

In this chapter, we are going to learn about StackSets—a part of CloudFormation that allows us to deploy stacks to different regions and accounts. StackSets are useful when it comes to managing big and enterprise-class infrastructure worldwide, whether you are hosting a software-as-a-service platform globally or are running distributed systems in AWS Cloud.

In this chapter, we will learn about StackSets and how to deploy them to multiple regions and accounts. By the end of this chapter, we will have learned how to prevent failures of multiple StackSet deployments using TAGs.

Before we dive into this, let's think about how we can perform stack operations in case we need to provision infrastructure to different accounts or regions.

We will cover the following topics in this chapter:

- The old-fashioned way of multi-regional and multi-account infrastructure management
- Introducing StackSets
- Deploying to multiple regions
- Best practices for StackSets
- Deploying to multiple accounts
- Preventing failures of multiple StackSet deployments using TAGs

Technical requirements

The code used in this chapter can be found in the book's GitHub repository at: `https://github.com/PacktPublishing/Mastering-AWS-CloudFormation/tree/master/Chapter5`

Check out the following video to see the Code in Action:

`https://bit.ly/3aTXgN4`

The old-fashioned way of multi-regional and multi-account infrastructure management

Until now, our stack deployment was primarily focused on provisioning resources within a single AWS account and region. But what if we need to provision the same stack in several regions? Let's say we need to provision the same stack in Ireland, North Virginia, and Frankfurt?

Usually, the default region (for example, the API endpoint that we want to connect to) is chosen either from environment variables or from a local config file. When you invoke any command via `awscli`, it will connect to that specific default region.

We can also specify the region manually as an argument. So, if we want to provision the same stack in different regions, we have to repeat the same command that changes the argument value:

```
aws cloudformation deploy --region eu-west-1 --template-file
foo.yaml
```
```
aws cloudformation deploy --region us-east-1 --template-file
foo.yaml
```
```
aws cloudformation deploy --region eu-central-1 --template-file
foo.yaml
```

But that brings us extra complexity. What if one of the deployments fails? If one stack is provisioned for more than 30 minutes, then the whole operation will take hours!

We might also need to deploy the same stack to multiple accounts. We will have to store multiple credentials and profiles in our local configuration file for awscli and specify the profiles one by one!

```
aws cloudformation deploy --profile dev
```
```
aws cloudformation deploy --profile test
```
```
aws cloudformation deploy --profile prod
```

And again, we have the same issue as we had with the regions.

AWS has a feature called *nested stacks*. We're not going to cover them in this book, because this is a legacy feature and maintaining nested stacks requires a lot of effort, but I think it is good for you to know about this concept.

Nested stacks is a feature of CloudFormation that allows the template developer to specify the CloudFormation stack as a resource in the CloudFormation template. The initial idea was to have a workaround for AWS's limits on the amount of resources per stack, but now nested stacks can also be used for this particular case. For more information, you can read AWS's blog at https://aws.amazon.com/blogs/infrastructure-and-automation/multiple-account-multiple-region-aws-cloudformation/.

In the end, the CloudFormation development team introduced a feature called *StackSets*, which solves all these problems. Let's dive into it.

Introducing StackSets

The result of CloudFormation stack deployment is always a bunch of resources, grouped in a single stack. StackSets can be deployed to target regions or even accounts (whether in your AWS organization or just a separate account), as shown in the following diagram:

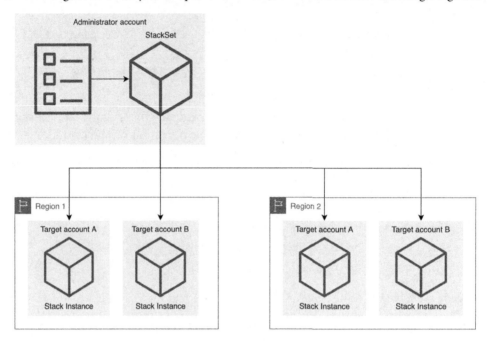

Figure 5.1 – StackSet architecture

As you can see in the preceding picture, each StackSet consists of one or more stacks, provisioned from the same template. Those stacks are referred to as stack instances and are distributed among various accounts and regions. This is the first concept that we need to know.

Another concept is administrator and target accounts. An administrator account is an account where StackSets are managed. Whenever we want to create or update StackSets, we need to use an administrator account. This account must be granted to create stacks in other accounts (which is handled by IAM). The accounts in which stacks are being created are target accounts.

If you want to use StackSets to provision stacks to different regions, but in a single account, then your administrator and target accounts will be the same.

If the creation of one of the stack instances fails, then that won't affect other stack instances.

Let's look at a simple case: you deploy a stack with resources from services that for now are not supported in some of AWS's regions. In those regions, the stack creation will obviously fail. CloudFormation, by design, will start to roll back the changes. We might think that all other stack instances will roll back too, but that's not going to happen. Only the affected stack instance will be reverted, while the others will be deployed with no issues. This behavior is maintained by failure tolerance, which we will cover in the next section.

> **Important note**
> If we delete a StackSet, then *all* of the stack instances should be deleted. In order to keep some of the stack instances, we need to delete them *from* the StackSet with an option to *retain*. That will remove the stack instance from the StackSet, but the stack on its own will stay.

That sounds complicated and increases the chance of accidental deletion. To prevent this from happening, AWS won't allow you to delete StackSet. First, you must delete the stack instances, and when the StackSet is *empty*, it can be deleted.

Yet another thing to know about StackSets is the so-called StackSet operation options.

While the StackSet operation terms are fairly simple (the operations are *create*, *update*, and *delete*), the options might be tricky.

StackSets deployments are based on rolling the update out of the box. To configure the deployment behavior, we can set the options to **maximum concurrent accounts**, **failure tolerance**, and **retain stacks**:

- **Maximum concurrent accounts** defines the amount of parallel deployments per account. That said, if we deploy five stack instances within a StackSet, then we can define the amount of concurrent deployments or a percentage. If we set this value to 2 (as a number) or 40 (as a percentage), then a deployment will occur in two accounts at the same time. Increasing this figure will improve the speed of stack provisioning, but if there is a mistake in a template that may lead to a failure, it will affect more target regions and accounts.

- **Failure tolerance** is an option that defines how we want to handle failure per deployment. This works only on a per-region basis and defines how many stack deployment failures we can ignore.

- **Retain stacks** is used only when we initiate the deletion of the stack instance from StackSet. We cannot delete StackSet when it's not empty. If we want to remove a stack instance from StackSet, but want to keep it in the target account or region, then we need to check this box.

The last thing to learn before we start is the permissions that we need to grant to the administrator and target accounts.

Permissions

Stack instances within a StackSet can be deployed only using CloudFormation service roles. At the same time, the administrator account must have a role that allows the creation of stack instances. Before we proceed, let's configure those permissions for our account.

> **Important note**
>
> StackSet management roles must have a name:
> `AWSCloudFormationStackSetAdministrationRole`
> for administrator accounts and
> `AWSCloudFormationStackSetExecutionRole` for target
> accounts. This is not a string, but is recommended, and is defined in the
> CloudFormation's documentation at `https://docs.aws.amazon.`
> `com/AWSCloudFormation/latest/UserGuide/stacksets-`
> `prereqs.html`.

To deploy these roles in our account (which will act as an administrator and target account at the same time), we will use the following:

CloudFormation:StackSetPermissions.yaml (administrator account)

```
StackSetAdministratorRole:
  Type: AWS::IAM::Role
  Properties:
    RoleName: "AWSCloudFormationStackSetAdministrationRole"
    AssumeRolePolicyDocument:
      # ...
    Policies:
      - PolicyName: StackSetAdministratorPolicy
        PolicyDocument:
          Version: 2012-10-17
          Statement:
            Effect: Allow
            Action: "sts:AssumeRole"
```

```
        Resource:
            - "arn:aws:iam::*:role/
AWSCloudFormationStackSetExecutionRole"
```

The administrator role only has one action that is allowed, and this is to assume the role in a target account:

StackSetPermissions.yaml (target account)

```
    StackSetExecutionRole:
      Type: AWS::IAM::Role
      Properties:
        RoleName: AWSCloudFormationStackSetExecutionRole
        AssumeRolePolicyDocument:
          Version: 2012-10-17
          Statement:
            Effect: Allow
            Action: "sts:AssumeRole"
            Principal:
              AWS: !Sub "arn:aws:iam::${AWS::AccountId}:root"
        ManagedPolicyArns:
          - "arn:aws:iam::aws:policy/AdministratorAccess"
```

The role in a target role will do all of the jobs, and so it must have enough permissions, so we grant administrator access to the execution role for the target account.

We also specify the `AWS::AccountId` pseudoparameter because for the next section, we will deploy StackSet in multiple regions, but in the same account, so we won't need to expose the AWS account ID in the template. We just need to deploy the stack using this template:

```
aws cloudformation deploy \
            --stack-name StackSet-Permissions \
            --template-file StackSetPermissions.yaml \
            --capabilities CAPABILITY_NAMED_IAM
```

Once stack is created, we are all set and ready to go. We've prepared IAM roles in order to allow StackSets to be created and provisioned. Now let's deploy our core stack to multiple regions!

Deploying to multiple regions

We are now going to start creating StackSet for a single account, but in multiple regions. We will begin with AWS Console.

Using AWS Console

Let's start by deploying StackSet with the core template in a single account (for example, our main account). We'll begin with AWS Console:

1. Once we log in to the console, we will go to **CloudFormation - StackSets** and click on **Create StackSet**. We will choose **Template is ready**, upload our core.yaml file (which you will find in the GitHub repository) and click **Next**. The template will be uploaded to S3 automatically:

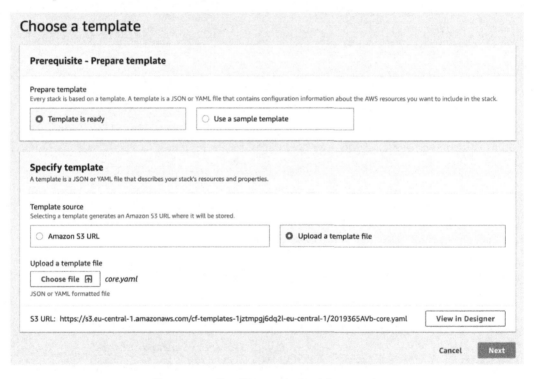

Figure 5.2 – CloudFormation StackSet console

2. Now we need to supply the StackSet name and parameters and hit **Next**:

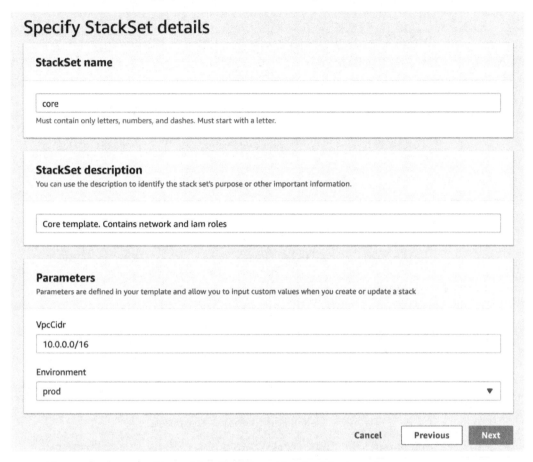

Figure 5.3 – CloudFormation StackSet console

> **Important note**
>
> We insert parameter values for the StackSet and these parameters will be inherited by stack instances. It is not yet possible to add unique parameters per stack instance during StackSet creation, since all stack instances by design are meant to be the same. Alternatively, we can create one stack instance for StackSet in the beginning, and then use `--parameter-overrides` when we add stack instances.

3. For this example, we are not going to provide any tags, but we must specify the administrator role for StackSet. We will leave the execution role unchanged and hit **Next**:

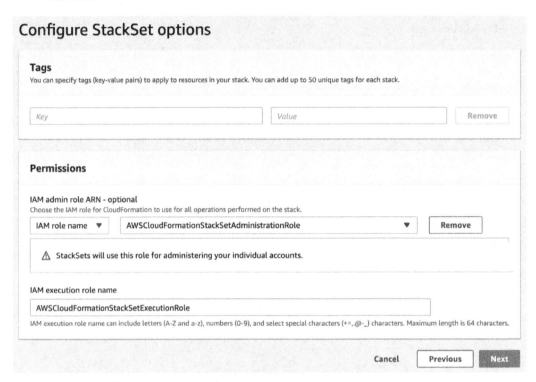

Figure 5.4 – CloudFormation StackSet console

4. Now we need to enter the values for AWS accounts, regions, and deployment options. Since we only create StackSet in our main accounts, we will choose **Deploy stacks in accounts** and add the account ID:

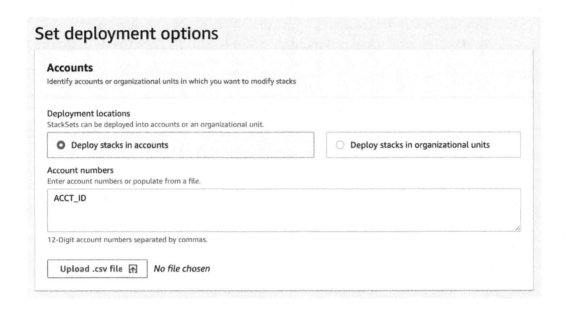

Figure 5.5 – CloudFormation StackSet console

5. Next, we need to specify the regions that we will deploy our stacks to. We will choose **North Virginia** (us-east-1) and **Ireland** (eu-west-1):

Figure 5.6 – CloudFormation StackSet console

We can change the order of regions if we wish, given that CloudFormation will deploy the stack instances in the order that they are specified in here. If we make Ireland our *test* region and N. Virginia our *prod* region, it will be wise to deploy first to test and then to production. But for this example, we will keep things as is.

Now let's look at our deployment options.

6. We will set **Maximum concurrent accounts** to **1** (since we will only deploy to our account) and **Failure tolerance** to **0**—we don't want to proceed if one of the stack instances fails to be provisioned. Then we hit **Next** one last time:

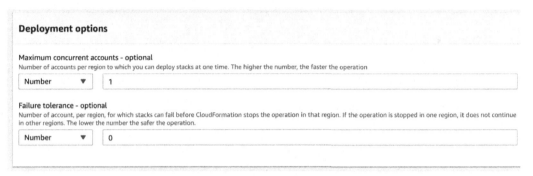

Figure 5.7 – CloudFormation StackSet console

7. We need to review the summary and check **I acknowledge that AWS CloudFormation might create IAM resources** (this is like setting CAPABILITY_ IAM in awscli). If there is something that we want to change, then we can click **Edit** on any of the steps in the **Summary**. If everything is set in order, then all we need to do is click **Submit**. Now we can review our StackSet:

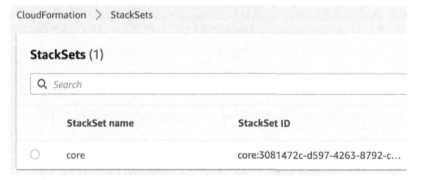

Figure 5.8 – CloudFormation StackSet console

In the StackSet information, we will see the summary and other properties of the StackSet. What we're interested in is *Stack Instances*:

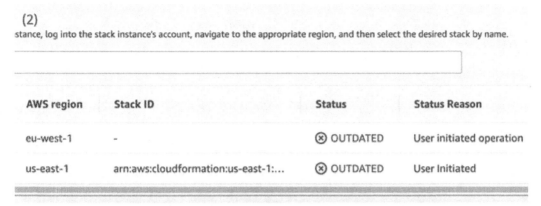

(2)

stance, log into the stack instance's account, navigate to the appropriate region, and then select the desired stack by name.

AWS region	Stack ID	Status	Status Reason
eu-west-1	-	⊗ OUTDATED	User initiated operation
us-east-1	arn:aws:cloudformation:us-east-1:...	⊗ OUTDATED	User Initiated

Figure 5.9 – CloudFormation StackSet console

8. We can see that only one stack is being provisioned. This is because we set **Maximum concurrent accounts** to **1** and deployment to Ireland will not begin until stack instance in N. Virginia is provisioned. We can't see CloudFormation events form this menu, so we will have to switch to the N. Virginia region and look them up there, as shown in the following screenshot:

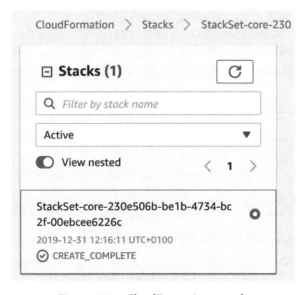

Figure 5.10 – CloudFormation console

9. We can see that this stack instance is created. Once both stack instances are created, we will see that their **Status** is **CURRENT** in the **Stack instances** section:

·g into the stack instance's account, navigate to the appropriate region, and then select the desired stack

AWS region	Stack ID	Status
eu-west-1	arn:aws:cloudf…	⊘ CURRENT
us-east-1	arn:aws:cloudf…	⊘ CURRENT

Figure 5.11 – CloudFormation StackSet console

Now, let's do the same using awscli. To clean up, we need to delete the stack instances from the StackSet and then the StackSet itself.

Using awscli

Creating StackSets using awscli introduces a few differences. One of them is that the creation of StackSet *and* stack instances is a different and independent operation. This means that we can easily use specific parameters per stack instance, which is helpful when we want to have slight changes in stack instances within a single StackSet.

By going through the following steps, we will be able to achieve multi region deployment:

1. We begin by creating a StackSet:

```
aws cloudformation create-stack-set \
                --stack-set-name core \
                --template-body file://core.yaml \
                --capabilities CAPABILITY_NAMED_IAM
```

We will see StackSetId in response. If we go to the AWS console, we will see the active StackSet with no stack instances; however, the parameters will be set (with the default values, unless we specify otherwise).

2. Now we create the first stack instance. We will still use our account, choose Ireland
    as the region, and override the parameters for `VpcCidr` and `Environment`:

```
$ aws cloudformation create-stack-instances \
                --stack-set-name core \
                --accounts ACCT_ID \
                --regions eu-west-1 \
                --parameter-overrides \
ParameterKey=VpcCidr,ParameterValue=10.1.0.0/16 \
ParameterKey=Environment,ParameterValue=test


# Response
{
    "OperationId": "7643d973-1358-475d-b148-5e096f9a44b9"
}
```

3. The `awscli` will return `OperationId`, and we can review our stack instance in
    the AWS Console or using the command-line interface:

```
$ aws cloudformation list-stack-instances --profile
personal --stack-set-name core

{
    "Summaries": [
        {
            "StackSetId": "core:ec0e8256-dcc9-4dd0-b074-
aee9721ed949",
            "Region": "eu-west-1",
            "Account": "ACCT_ID",
            "StackId": "arn:aws:cloudformation:eu-west-
1:ACCT_ID:stack/StackSet-core-f8b4d34b-abaf-4e97-b004-
9309ea693803/124e9400-2bc6-11ea-8c11-0abd335268a4",
            "Status": "OUTDATED",
            "StatusReason": "User Initiated",
            "DriftStatus": "NOT_CHECKED"
        }
    ]
}
```

4. We don't have to wait until this stack instance is created. Let's create the production stack instance:

```
aws cloudformation create-stack-instances \
                    --stack-set-name core \
                    --accounts ACCT_ID \
                    --regions us-east-1 \
                    --parameter-overrides \
ParameterKey=VpcCidr,ParameterValue=10.0.0.0/16 \
ParameterKey=Environment,ParameterValue=prod
```

Voila! Using `awscli`, we were able to work around the issue with inherited parameters from StackSets! Now let's check how StackSets work in a multi account environment.

Best practices for StackSets

Before we begin, we need to learn a bit about best practices for StackSets. This is crucial, because we don't want to make a monstrous zoo instead of a properly organized infrastructure, and we want to have efficiency and transparency for stack operations. The most important of these are listed as follows:

- **Develop universal templates**: By default, StackSet deploys the same template and parameter set in all the regions and accounts. To allow this process to be as automated as possible, we must focus on the reusability of our template. Do not hardcode regions and availability zones; instead, use AWS SSM parameter stores in every account and region to ease the deployment of StackSet. Don't set names for global resources such as IAM roles, users, groups, policies, S3 bucket, and so on to avoid naming conflicts.

  Think big, start small. If you are asked to create a StackSet for an application that will serve tens of accounts and regions, it is wise to start with only a few of them. Get some hands-on experience, improve your template, and continue growing.

- **Don't forget about deployment performance:**: It will take a lot of time to perform rolling updates on StackSet. You can speed up this process if you set your maximum concurrent operations accordingly.

- **Don't forget about validation and linting**: Even if StackSet will stop operation in case of failure and roll back, we don't want to slow down. Doing preflight checks using linting and validation will save us a lot of time.

Make sure you look up the best practices for StackSets in the AWS documentation (you will find the link in the *Further reading* section). Meanwhile, let's continue looking at how to deploy to multiple accounts.

Deploying to multiple accounts

Now let's begin working with multiple accounts. For this section, I've created two additional accounts in AWS Organizations: testing and production.

> **Important note**
>
> Since this book is not about **multi-account strategies** (**MAS**), we're not going to cover the creation of child accounts and organizational units in this book. If you need to learn about these, then you can start looking at AWS Organizations (https://aws.amazon.com/organizations/). If you don't use a multi-account strategy and don't plan to, then you may skip this section.

Since we will work in various accounts, we need to tweak our StackSet permissions template. We've separated it into two templates—one for administrator role and one for an execution role. We don't need to create an execution role in our main (or to use the terms of AWS, our payer) account, because no stack instance will be created in it.

Our StackSet administrator role is the same, but the StackSet execution role will be a bit different:

StackSetExecution.yaml

```
AWSTemplateFormatVersion: "2010-09-09"
Description: StackSet IAM roles
Parameters:
  AdministratorAccountId:
    Type: String
    AllowedPattern: "(\d+)$"
Resources:
  StackSetExecutionRole:
    Type: AWS::IAM::Role
    Properties:
      # ...
          Principal:
            AWS:
```

```
      Fn::Join:
        - ""
        - - "arn:aws:iam::"
          - !Ref AdministratorAccountId
          - ":root"
# ...
```

Here, we add a `AdministratorAccountId` parameter, which we will enter manually. This parameter will be used to set a proper `Principal` for the execution role.

To deploy this stack in all the child accounts, we will add an API key and secret to `~/.aws/credentials` under different profiles and use those profiles to provision execution roles:

```
$ aws cloudformation deploy \
                --stack-name Admin-Role \
                --template-file StackSetAdmin.yaml \
                --capabilities CAPABILITY_NAMED_IAM
$ aws cloudformation deploy \
                --stack-name Exec-Role \
                --profile test \
                --template-file StackSetExec.yaml \
                --parameter-overrides \
                AdministratorAccountId=ACCT_ID \
                --capabilities CAPABILITY_NAMED_IAM
$ aws cloudformation deploy \
                --stack-name Exec-Role \
                --profile prod \
                --template-file StackSetExec.yaml \
                --parameter-overrides \
                AdministratorAccountId=ACCT_ID \
                --capabilities CAPABILITY_NAMED_IAM
```

Once it's done, we can start by creating a StackSet with multiple accounts. We've altered our core template as well: now it will have a single `VpcCidr`, which defaults to `10.0.0.0/16`, as we don't expect our production and testing environment to interact with each other and have removed the `Environment` parameter since we separated testing and production on the AWS account level. This will reduce the number of steps we need to take when we deploy StackSets across different accounts.

Following the preceding steps, we will deploy a multi account infrastructure:

1. Again, we first create a StackSet:

```
aws cloudformation create-stack-set \
                --stack-set-name core \
                --template-body file://core.yaml \
                --capabilities CAPABILITY_NAMED_IAM
```

2. Then we create stack instances, but this time, we will change the arguments a bit. First, we will specify two child accounts, testing and production, and set Maximum concurrent operations to 100% in order to deploy to both accounts in parallel:

```
aws cloudformation create-stack-instances \
                --stack-set-name core \
                --accounts ACCT_ID_PROD ACCT_ID_TEST \
                --regions REGION \
                --operation-preferences \
MaxConcurrentPercentage=100
```

One thing we need to remember is that the number of concurrent deployments is defined per account per region. This means that if we work with two accounts and three regions, then the first batch will be done in one account, then another, and then in the third.

Let's move on to the next topic.

Preventing failures of multiple StackSet deployments using TAGs

When we want to deploy StackSets where stack instances in one StackSet depend on the stack instances in another , then we need to make sure that these deployments do not fail.

Although there is a failure-tolerance option in implementing StackSet operations, we need to catch and handle all possible exceptions before the actual operation.

StackSets have an optional feature called a target account gate. A **target account gate** (**TAG**) is a Lambda function that is executed on a target account before a StackSet operation and checks whether a target account is *ready* to perform this operation—for example, if the required resources exist, or if there is no other ongoing StackSet operation.

TAGs must be developed by us, but their outcome is quite simple: if all checks pass, then it should return SUCCESS, or FAIL if one or more checks do not pass.

For this chapter, we will develop a TAG function that will check the following:

- Whether a core stack exists
- Whether the necessary exports from the core stack also exist
- Whether the SSH key exists on EC2

We need this because we will deploy WebTier StackSet on top of the core StackSet. As we remember from *Chapter 2, Advanced Template Development*, WebTier resources are created in subnets, which are a part of the core stack.

Since our TAG will invoke CloudFormation's and EC2's API, it must have an IAM role, which allows `Get*` and `Describe*` calls to those services.

We will deploy our TAG function in a single-account environment (to make it possible for those readers who do not yet use multi account strategies and AWS Organizations).

> **Important note**
> The TAG function must have a name like
> `AWSCloudFormationStackSetAccountGate`. While it is possible
> to override the default names for the StackSet administrator and execution role,
> it is not yet possible to set a custom name for TAG. If the TAG function name is
> different, or this function cannot be invoked, StackSet will ignore TAG's check.

Our TAG will have a handler (which is a `"main"` function for Lambda) and three functions:

```
check_if_key_exists,
check_if_core_stack_exists,
check_if_exports_exist.
```

Our script should look like the following.

This function below connects to the EC2 service and checks whether the SSH key `"mykey"` is present:

tag.py

```
import boto3
def check_if_key_exists():
    client = boto3.client('ec2')
    try:
        resp = client.describe_key_pairs(KeyNames=["mykey"])
    except Exception:
```

```
        return False
    if len(resp['KeyPairs']) == 0:
        return False
    return True
```

This function connects to the CloudFormation service and requests information on the core stack:

tag.py

```
def check_if_core_stack_exists():
    client = boto3.client('cloudformation')
    try:
        resp = client.describe_stacks(StackName="core")
    except Exception:
        return False
    if len(resp['Stacks']) == 0:
        return False
    return True
```

This function connects to the CloudFormation service too, but runs a different API call to obtain exported outputs:

tag.py

```
def check_if_exports_exist():
    to_check = ["WebTierSubnet1Id",
                'WebTierSubnet2Id',
                "WebTierSubnet3Id",
                "VpcId",
                "WebTierMaxSizeParameter",
                "WebTierMinSizeParameter",
                "WebTierDesSizeParameter"]
    exports = []
    client = boto3.client('cloudformation')
    try:
        resp = client.list_exports()
    except Exception:
```

```
        return False
    for export in resp['Exports']:
        exports.append(export['Name'])
    if not all(exp in exports for exp in to_check):
        return False
    return True
```

Lastly, the Lambda handler, which will invoke all the functions above tag.py:

```
def lambda_handler(event, context):
    status = "SUCCEEDED"
    if not (check_if_key_exists() and check_if_core_stack_
exists() and check_if_exports_exist()):
        status = "FAILED"
    return {
        'Status': status
    }
```

As we can see in the lambda_handler function, if any of those functions return False, then the TAG result is FAILED.

Let's package our TAG into the CloudFormation template:

tag.yaml

```yaml
AWSTemplateFormatVersion: "2010-09-09"
Resources:
  AccountGateFunctionRole:
    Type: 'AWS::IAM::Role'
    Properties:
      # ...
  AccountGateFunction:
    Type: 'AWS::Lambda::Function'
    Properties:
      FunctionName: 'AWSCloudFormationStackSetsAccountGate'
      Code:
        ZipFile: |
          # source code of our function...
      Handler: lambda_function.lambda_handler
```

```
MemorySize: 128
Runtime: python3.7
Timeout: 30
Role: !GetAtt AccountGateFunctionRole.Arn
```

Now we just need to deploy this TAG:

```
aws cloudformation deploy \
                --stack-name tag \
                --template-file tag.yaml \
                --capabilities CAPABILITY_IAM
```

Note, that the TAG function must be deployed in every account *and* region where stack instances will be created. Once the TAG stack is deployed, we can create a StackSet for WebTier (the same way we did before for the core StackSet).

```
aws cloudformation create-stack-set \
                --stack-set-name webtier \
                --template-body file://webtier.yaml
aws cloudformation create-stack-instances \
                --stack-set-name webtier \
                --accounts ACCT_ID \
                --regions eu-central-1
```

What we will see is obviously an error:

Status	Status Reason
⊗ OUTDATED	AccountGate check failed

Figure 5.12 – CloudFormation StackSet console

This is because the core stack doesn't exist.

Checking by TAG doesn't show enough information, as we can see here (try to find out which check failed exactly. The first thing it looks up is the TAG function logs.), but it can help us to prevent failures before the StackSet operations initiate, thereby protecting us from unexpected downtime.

What we also must remember is that TAG is only done during create and update operations and *not* for the deletion of stack instances.

Summary

In this chapter, we've learned about StackSets, their use cases, how to deploy them, and how to work with failures.

StackSets are a promising feature, although they introduce some complexity, and it is not easy to integrate them with continuous delivery systems. Nevertheless, they come in handy when you want to provision the same stacks across multiple regions or even accounts.

Consider using StackSets when you are tasked to deploy the same environment and resources to your customers—for example, if you provide a B2B SaaS platform or want to automate deployment for development, test, staging, and production environments. StackSets are also useful for replicating your applications across multiple regions if you need to have a point of presence in various countries and continents.

In the next chapter, we will use `cfn-init`, CloudFormation's helper script, to install software on EC2 resources. Stay tuned!

Questions

1. Is it possible to have custom names for administrator and execution roles?

2. If you create a StackSet in a single account, is it possible to create stack instances in multiple regions at the same time?

3. In which order are stack instances created?

4. Is it possible to delete a StackSet if it has stack instances in it?

5. What are the required actions allowed for the administrator IAM role in StackSet?

Further reading

- StackSets best practices: `https://docs.aws.amazon.com/AWSCloudFormation/latest/UserGuide/stacksets-bestpractices.html`

- Target account gate: `https://docs.aws.amazon.com/AWSCloudFormation/latest/UserGuide/stacksets-account-gating.html`

6
Configuration Management of the EC2 Instances Using cfn-init

There are multiple ways to manage the configuration of your EC2 instances and applications on AWS. There is `user-data`, a basic shell script that runs during the launch of an EC2 instance. You can use configuration management systems, such as Ansible, Puppet, Chef, and SaltStack, to manage your resources. AWS provides a service called *OpsWorks*—a managed Chef or Puppet server.

We are going to learn about `cfn-init` (CloudFormation's own configuration management tool) and how can we use it to deploy applications on EC2 resources. We are going to cover `cfn-init` along with `AWS::CloudFormation:Init`, CloudFormation's metadata key, which actually declares configuration items for EC2 resources.

In this chapter, we will cover the following topics:

- Introducing `cfn-init`
- Deploying your application on EC2 during stack creation
- Using `cfn-signal` to inform CloudFormation of resource readiness

Technical requirements

The code used in this chapter can be found in the book's GitHub repository at: `https://github.com/PacktPublishing/Mastering-AWS-CloudFormation/tree/master/Chapter6`

Check out the following video to see the Code in Action:

`https://bit.ly/2xpOhpk`

Introducing cfn-init

CloudFormation is a declarative instrument. This means that everything in your template is a declaration of what should be there in CloudFormation's state. And since you use resource attributes to declare your infrastructure, you must store your configuration in it as well, whether it's a source code in a Lambda function or `user-data` in an EC2 launch template, launch configuration, or instance.

Using `user-data` is a very simple process, but it is hard to declare a configuration in it. In the end, you will do a lot of shell programming, which is not as reliable as configuration management should be.

Luckily, CloudFormation has a set of so-called *helper scripts*—instruments that can get the data from CloudFormation's metadata or a stack, process it and perform operations on your resources. One of them is called `cfn-init`.

> **Important note**
> The `cfn-init` instrument (and any other helper script) is only included in Amazon Linux AMIs as a part of the distribution. For other Linux or Windows distributions, you will have to install it first. For more information, read the documentation about helper scripts from AWS at `https://docs.aws.amazon.com/AWSCloudFormation/latest/UserGuide/cfn-helper-scripts-reference.html`.

EC2 instances support bootstrapping for initial configuration and software installation. This bootstrapping is called `user-data`, a simple Bash script that runs under the root user as soon as an instance is up.

How is `cfn-init` actually applied to user-data? It is simply added to the user-data block in a resource declaration. For example, we can instruct our EC2 resource to run `cfn-init` by adding the command and arguments as shown in the following code:

```
UserData: !Base64
  'Fn::Join':
    - ''
    - - |
        #!/bin/bash -xe
      - |
        # Install the files and packages from the metadata
      - '/opt/aws/bin/cfn-init -v '
      - '          --stack '
      - !Ref 'AWS::StackName'
      - '          --resource MyInstance '
      - '          --configsets DeploySoftware '
      - '          --region '
      - !Ref 'AWS::Region'
      - |+
```

In the preceding code snippet, we can see that the root user will run the `cfn-init` command, providing the necessary arguments to it, such as the stack name, the resource to refer to and ConfigSets, and the AWS region.

But where is this data obtained from? Looking at the arguments, we might notice that `cfn-init` is attempting to talk to a stack.

You might remember that in *Chapter 2, Advanced Template Development*, we looked at stack or resource **metadata**. Metadata contains specific details about our resources or the entire stack. The metadata has specific keys, and one such key that we are going to work with is called `AWS::CloudFormation::Init`.

This `AWS::CloudFormation::Init` (for simplicity, I'm going to call it just init) metadata can be included only in EC2 resources, such as instance, launch configuration, or a launch template.

Init is a simplified configuration-management system that can carry out the following actions on the EC2 resource:

- Run commands
- Write files to disk (for example, configuration files)
- Create groups
- Create users
- Install packages
- Start, enable, and stop services
- Download data from various sources (GitHub or S3)

Let's say that we want to install and run an Apache web server on an EC2 instance. To set this up, our init metadata should look like the following:

```
Web server:
  Type: AWS::EC2::Instance
  Metadata:
    AWS::CloudFormation::Init:
      configSets:
      - "Deploy"
      Deploy:
        InstallAndRun:
          packages:
            yum:
              httpd: []
          services:
          # this is a key for init metadata.
          # cfn-init will use init.d or systemd if necessary
            sysvinit:
              httpd:
                enabled: "true"
                ensureRunning: "true"
```

Here, we declare init in the resource's metadata and use two keys for init: `packages` and `services`. These keys (for example, the actions to be done) are declared under ConfigSet `InstallAndRun`. Now all we need to do is add `cfn-init` to the `UserData` block:

```
Webserver:
  Type: AWS::EC2::Instance
  # Metadata block…
  Properties:
  # some properties…
    UserData: !Base64:
      Fn::Join:
        - ""
        - - |
              #!/bin/bash -xe
          - |
          - "/opt/aws/bin/cfn-init -v "
          - " --stack "
          - !Ref "AWS::StackName"
          - "--resource Webserver"
          - " --configsets Deploy --region "
          - !Ref "AWS::Region"
          - |+
```

This block will make our instance talk to CloudFormation's API to obtain its metadata and run all the necessary configurations.

> **Important note**
>
> You've probably noticed that we specify the region (because by default, the underlying OS doesn't know which region it belongs to), but we don't provide any API key/secret or IAM role ARN. The `cfn-init` tool doesn't need an IAM role to talk to CloudFormation's resource metadata because it authenticates CloudFormation again by checking that this *physical* resource is actually a member of this CloudFormation stack.

We've covered the basics of `cfn-init`, but there is a lot more that CloudFormation's helper scripts can do. Let's learn about them by going through some examples.

Deploying your application to EC2 during stack creation

In this section, we will get hands-on experience with `cfn-init` by using it to bootstrap an application on EC2 instances.

We will begin with a simple Hello, World example.

Creating a Hello, World application

We'll start by implementing a basic Hello, World application, which is going to be deployed in an `AutoScaling` group. This is going to be an application based on Flask—a lightweight Python web framework:

1. Let's develop our app:

---

hello-world-flask.py

```python
#!/usr/bin/env python3

from flask import Flask
app = Flask(__name__)

@app.route("/")
def hello():
    return "Hello, World, from AWS!"

if __name__ == "__main__":
    app.run(host="0.0.0.0", port=80)
```

Nothing really serious. We will store this application on S3 and use `cfn-init` to install Python and Flask, pull the code from S3, create a SystemD unit, and start a service that will serve our application.

2. Let's develop our templates. We'll need a preparation template (an S3 bucket and network) to store the Python script and have the network configured:

hello-world-prep.yaml

```
AWSTemplateFormatVersion: "2010-09-09"
Description: HelloWorld prep template
Parameters:
  VpcCidr:
    Type: String
    AllowedPattern: '(\d{1,3})\.(\d{1,3})\.(\d{1,3})\.
(\d{1,3})/(\d{1,2})'
Resources:
  SourceBucket: # …
  Vpc: # …
  Igw: # …
  IgwAttachment: # …
  Subnet1: # …
  Subnet2: # …
  PublicRouteTable: # …
  PublicRoute: # …
  PublicRtAssoc1: # …
  PublicRtAssoc2: # …
Outputs:
  VpcId: #...
  Subnet1Id: #...
  Subnet2Id: #...
```

Here, we declare our required resources with properties and necessary exports that we'll use in the next template. Let's deploy this template to the stack:

```
aws cloudformation deploy \
                --stack-name hello-world-prep \
                --template-file hello-world-prep.yaml
```

Now we need to develop our application resources template. We've already done this a couple of times, so I'm going to show only the important bits in the following steps.

To run our application, we'll need an Elastic load balancer, launch configuration, AutoScaling group, an IAM role and a few security groups:

1. We will start with the IAM role:

hello-world-app.yaml

```
AppRole:
  Type: AWS::IAM::Role
  Properties:
    AssumeRolePolicyDocument:
      Version: "2012-10-17"
      Statement:
        - Effect: Allow
          Action: "sts:AssumeRole"
          Principal:
            Service: "ec2.amazonaws.com"
    Policies:
      - PolicyName: S3
        PolicyDocument:
          Version: "2012-10-17"
          Statement:
            - Effect: Allow
              Action: "s3:*"
              Resource: "*"
```

We already know that cfn-init can access CloudFormation to retrieve metadata, but we need an instance to be able to pull the source code of our app from S3, and that's why we add this role.

2. We store two metadata keys for our launch configuration. The first one is AWS::CloudFormation::Authentication:

hello-world-app.yaml

```
AWS::CloudFormation::Authentication:
  role:
    type: "S3"
    buckets:
```

```
      - !ImportValue S3Bucket
    roleName: !Ref AppRole
```

This block declares that `cfn-init` will use the IAM role to authenticate against S3. The second metadata key is `AWS::CloudFormation::Init`. It contains several elements:

hello-world-app.yaml

```
AWS::CloudFormation::Init:
  configSets:
    InstallAndRun:
      - "Configure"
  Configure:
    # …
```

Here, we declare ConfigSets, the configuration blocks (only one in this case) that will be applied by `cfn-init`. The `InstallAndRun` config set has only one configuration item, which is called `Configure`.

It contains the actions that need to be taken, which we will look at in the following steps.

3. The first action will be to install packages:

hello-world-app.yaml

```
packages:
  yum:
    python3: []
    python3-pip: []
```

Here, we declare which packages we want to install. Since our application is based on Python 3 and requires an external dependency to be installed (Flask), we install `python3` and `python3-pip`, since they are not included in the base distribution.

4. Next, we add the actual application files:

hello-world-app.yaml

```
files:
  /opt/helloworld.py:
    owner: root
```

```
    group: root
    mode: 755
    source: !Join ["", ["https://", !ImportValue
S3Bucket, ".s3.", !Ref "AWS::Region", ".", !Ref
"AWS::URLSuffix", "/hello-world-flask.py" ]]
    authentification: "role"
  /etc/systemd/system/helloworld.service:
    owner: root
    group: root
    mode: 755
    content: |
      [Unit]
      Description=HelloWorld service
      After=network.target
      [Service]
      Type=simple
      User=root
      ExecStart=/opt/helloworld.py
      Restart=on-abort
      [Install]
      WantedBy=multi-user.target
```

There are two files that we will create. The first one (/opt/helloworld.py) is the source code of our application and is retrieved from S3. Here, we supply the authentication element called "role". This will instruct cfn-init to assume our IAM role in order to obtain the object from S3.

The second one is the SystemD unit, which is added to the systemd directory to register a service.

5. Lastly, we add the commands section with the commands and services in order to install Flask, reload SystemD, and start our application as a service:

```
commands:
  installflask:
    # This commands runs installation
    command: "pip3 install flask"
    # This commands runs BEFORE command above
    # and checks if pip3 is present on system
    # if return code is not 0 cfn-init stops
```

```
test: "which pip3"
  reloadsystemd:
    command: "systemctl daemon-reload"
services:
  sysvinit:
    helloworld:
      enabled: "true"
      ensureRunning: "true"
```

6. Now we are ready to deploy our application stack, but before we do this, we need to upload the source to S3:

```
$ aws s3 ls
2020-01-13 16:26:31 hello-world-prep-sourcebucket-
1615b2vvpr5js
$ aws s3 cp hello-world-flask.py s3://hello-world-prep-
sourcebucket-1615b2vvpr5js
upload: ./hello-world-flask.py to s3://hello-world-prep-
sourcebucket-1615b2vvpr5js/hello-world-flask.py
$ aws cloudformation deploy \
                    --stack-name helloworld \
                    --template-file hello-world-app.yaml
\
                    --capabilities CAPABILITY_IAM
```

Once the stack is deployed, we can send an HTTP request to the **Elastic load balancer (ELB)**:

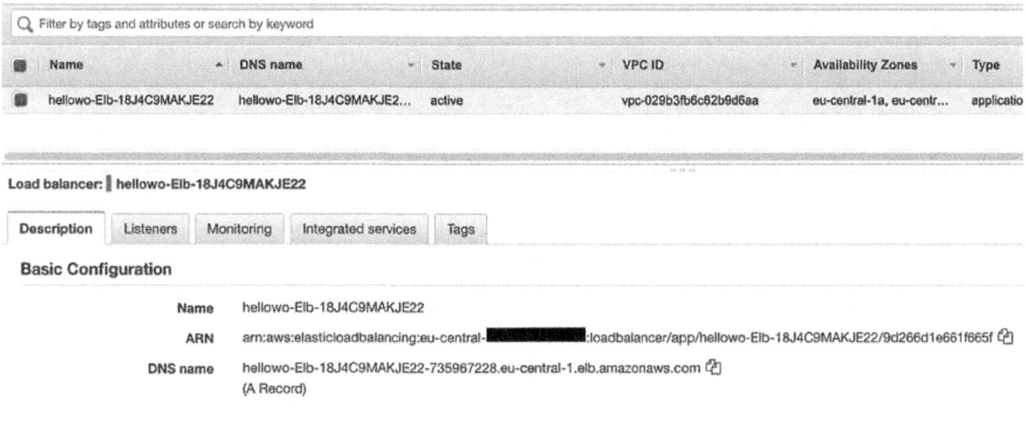

Figure 6.1 – AWS EC2 ELB Console

We can check the code by running `curl` against our ELB DNS name:

```
$ curl hellowo-Elb-18J4C9MAKJE22-735967228.eu-central-1.
elb.amazonaws.com
Hello, World, from AWS!
```

We're all set! Now let's try to build something bigger than just a small web app. How about an LNMP (Linux, NGINX, MySQL, PHP) stack?

Creating LNMP stack

Since most LNMP stacks are a single-node installation, we will install a single EC2 instance and declare all of its configuration in the metadata. We will use AWS's provided demo PHP app to check that our LNMP stack is operational.

Going through the following steps, we will have an LNMP stack running with a sample application:

1. We will start by declaring an EC2 instance. It will look like this:

lnmp.yaml

```yaml
Resources:
  Lnmp:
    Type: AWS::EC2::Instance
    Properties:
      ImageId: !Ref ImageId
      InstanceType: t2.micro
      KeyName: !Ref KeyName
      UserData:
        Fn::Base64:
          Fn::Join:
            - ""
            - - |
                  #!/bin/bash -xe
              - |
                - "/opt/aws/bin/cfn-init -v "
                - " --stack "
                - !Ref "AWS::StackName"
                - " --resource Lnmp"
```

```
            - " --configsets Configure --region "
            - !Ref "AWS::Region"
            - |+
```

Since we need to perform more actions and configurations this time, we'll use multiple configuration items. Configuring the config set will consist of setting up MySQL, PHP, and NGINX setup. So our metadata skeleton should look like this:

```
Metadata:
  AWS::CloudFomration:Init:
    configSets:
      Configure:
        - "Mysql"
        - "DbSetup"
        - "Php"
        - "Nginx"
```

2. Let's start with the MySQL installation and database setup. We'll install the necessary packages, run the service, and create the user and database. The setup process is similar to what we did before, so I'd like to point to few new things here:

lnmp.yaml

```
files:
  #...
  /etc/cfn/cfn-hup.conf:
    content: !Sub |
      [main]
      stack=${AWS::StackId}
      region=${AWS::Region}
    mode: 400
    owner: root
    group: root
  /etc/cfn/hooks.d/cfn-auto-reloader.conf:
    content: !Sub |
      [cfn-auto-reloader-hook]
      triggers=post.update
      path=Resources.Lnmp.Metadata.
AWS::CloudFormation::Init
```

```
action=#...
runas=root
```

Let me introduce you to `cfn-hup`, `cfn-init`'s little helper! The `cfn-init` tool is declarative, so each time we update the metadata, we need to recreate the resource, which can be achieved *within* the AutoScaling group and update policies, but it is troublesome to do this with stateful systems.

The `cfn-hup` tool has its own configuration file, which dictates the stack that we store the information in and the region that we should look into, and it has specific hooks. Hooks are used to look into the changes in the resource's metadata (as we pointed out in the preceding template) and run a specific action. An action is a bash command, so we can implement automation. In our case, we will rerun `cfn-init`. The `cfn-hup` phrase has to run as a service, so we must not forget to include it in the `services` section!

Another important thing to not is the following code fragment, where we add numbers before the command steps:

lnmp.yaml

```
commands:
  01_set_mysql_root_pw:
    command: #...
  02_create_database:
    command: #...
    test: #...
```

So why add numbering to the commands? The trick is that commands in the `commands` section run *not* in the declaration order, but in *alphabetical* order! That's why we need to add numbers at the start of each command step if one command needs to run after another.

We also ensure that both MySQL and `cfn-hup` are running:

lnmp.yaml

```
services:
  sysvinit:
    mariadb:
      enabled: True
```

```
      ensureRunning: True
  cfn-hup:
    enabled: True
    ensureRunning: True
    files:
      - "/etc/cfn/cfn-hup.conf"
      - "/etc/cfn/hooks.d/cfn-auto-reloader.conf"
```

We will also make sure that `cfn-hup` *watches* its own files and restarts if there is a change in it.

3. The PHP and Nginx setup are going to be similar, but we will run them separately. The reason why we want to separate these configurations is that Nginx is our actual frontend. Before starting the frontend, we want to have the backend (MySQL) and middleware operational:

lnmp.yaml

```
  Php:
    packages:
      yum:
        php: []
        php-mysql: []
        php-fpm: []
    files:
      /var/www/html/index.php:
        content: !Sub |
          # a lot of PHP and HTML here...
        mode: 644
        owner: root
        group: root
    services:
      sysvinit:
        php-fpm:
          enabled: True
          ensureRunning: True
```

4. The next and the last bit is our web server. We will add configuration files to Nginx and make sure that the Nginx service is running:

lnmp.yaml

```
Nginx:
  packages:
    yum:
      nginx: []
  files:
    /etc/nginx/nginx.conf:
      content: !Sub |
        # ...
    /etc/nginx/conf.d/default.conf:
      content: !Sub |
        # ...
  services:
    sysvinit:
      nginx:
        enabled: True
        ensureRunning: True
```

5. Once it's done, we can deploy our stack:

```
aws cloudformation deploy \
            --stack-name lnmp \
            --template-file lnmp.yaml \
            --parameter-overrides \
            DBName=foo \
            DBUsername=bar \
            DBPassword=foobar123 \
            DBRootPassword=barfoo321
```

6. Then we send an HTTP request to our web server:

```
$ aws cloudformation describe-stacks --stack-name lnmp
--profile personal | jq .[][].Outputs[].OutputValue
"http://ec2-18-194-210-115.eu-central-1.compute.
amazonaws.com"
```

```
$ curl http://ec2-18-194-210-115.eu-central-1.compute.
amazonaws.com
# super lengthy response...
```

And that's it! We have fully configured our LNMP stack, which listens to the changes in CloudFormation stack's metadata and will rerun `cfn-init` if there are any. There is one last thing we need to learn before finishing this chapter.

Using cfn-signal to inform CloudFormation about resource readiness

CloudFormation reports resource readiness as soon as it retrieves a response from AWS's API that the resource is created. By this, we understand that if we create an RDS instance and CloudFormation tells us that it's created, then we can connect to it right away.

While this is applicable for most of the managed services at AWS, it doesn't work on services that we run based on EC2. You see, CloudFormation is *not aware* that EC2 has a job to run and reports *Done* once the instance is in a *Running* state.

For small development environments this might be fine, but imagine running a web application on an AutoScaling group. While the instance takes time to install packages and start services, AutoScaling reports that the instance is unhealthy and terminates it. A new one starts, time passes, and then gets terminated. The worst thing here is that CloudFormation will tell you that your AutoScaling group is ready while your applications are still down.

In order to report EC2 resource readiness, there is a helper script called `cfn-signal`. This script (as it states in its name) sends signal message to CloudFormation reporting whether a resource has been created or has failed to be created.

Let try this with our LNMP stack. We'll need to add two additional blocks:

1. We start by adding *CreationPolicy* to the EC2 instance:

lnmp-signal.yaml

```
Lnmp:
  Type: AWS::EC2::Instance
  CreationPolicy:
    ResourceSignal:
      Count: 1
      Timeout: PT5M
```

```
Properties: #...
Metadata: #...
```

For individual instances, `CreationPolicy` doesn't have many attributes—only `Count` and `Timeout`.

`Timeout` is declared using the ISO8601 (https://www.iso.org/iso-8601-date-and-time-format.html) duration format and in the preceding example, this is five minutes. If CloudFormation doesn't receive any signal from an instance, it will report failure because of timeout and roll back.

But that's only for a declaration in CloudFormation. We also need to instruct our instance to report readiness.

2. The `cfn-signal` is already preinstalled on the machine, so we need to invoke it from `UserData`:

lnmp-signal.yaml

```yaml
Lnmp:
  Type: AWS::EC2::Instance
  CreationPolicy: #...
  Properties:
    ImageId: !Ref ImageId
    InstanceType: t2.micro
    KeyName: !Ref KeyName
    UserData:
      Fn::Base64:
        Fn::Sub: |
          #!/bin/bash -xe
          /opt/aws/bin/cfn-init -v \
          --stack ${AWS::StackName} \
          --resource Lnmp \
          --configsets Configure \
          --region ${AWS::Region}
          # signal creation
          /opt/aws/bin/cfn-signal -e $? \
          --stack ${AWS::StackName} \
          --resource Lnmp \
          --region ${AWS::Region}
```

Here, we supply CloudFormation with an exit code (the `-e` argument), the value of which equals the exit code of `cfn-init`. If `cfn-init` fails (if the exit code is not 0), then `cfn-signal` will send a different value to CloudFormation, and CloudFormation will know: Something went wrong, I should roll back.

Both `cfn-signal` and CreationPolicies are widely used with AutoScaling groups, since we can also specify `MinSuccessfulInstancesPercent`, thereby performing rolling updates.

See the following, for example:

```
MyAsg:
    Type: AWS::AutoScaling::AutoScalingGroup
    CreationPolicy:
        AutoScalingCreationPolicy:
            MinSuccessfulInstancePercent: 50
```

This declaration will instruct the AutoScaling group to confirm its readiness only if at least half of the group's members send success signals; otherwise, the AutoScaling group will report as having failed to be created.

Summary

In this chapter, we learned how to perform an initial bootstrap configuration in a more human-friendly way. We learned about `cfn-init`, CloudFormation's native configuration-management tool. We used it to deploy a Hello, World application and we even launched our own LNMP stack and instructed it to report its creation status to us.

Using `cfn-init` allows template developers to use CloudFormation as a centralized tool to both provision resources and underlying configurations and deploy them. `cfn-init` can be also used to install and update software as a part of the stack operations.

This is the last chapter in *Part 2, Provisioning and Deployment at Scale*, and we've done a lot of work here. We are now capable of building production-ready infrastructures with CloudFormation, we can test and validate our stacks, we can apply continuous delivery, and we can deploy our stacks in multiple regions and accounts using StackSets.

We did a lot of work mostly utilizing core CloudFormation features, but CloudFormation is also capable of extension using powerful tools such as custom resources and template macros. In the next few chapters, we will learn how to use these.

Moreover, we will also dive into the potential successors of CloudFormation: Serverless Application Model and AWS CDK—Cloud Development Kit.

In the next chapter, we will look at custom resources, CloudFormation's extension that allows us to declare and create resources *outside* of AWS. We will learn about custom resources and how and when to use them.

Stay tuned!

Questions

1. If the configuration set has multiple configuration items, in which order are they executed?

2. Is it possible to have multiple configuration sets?

3. Does `cfn-init` require the IAM policy to reach resource metadata?

4. Is it possible to create a directory with `cfn-init`?

5. What is a *WaitCondition*?

Further reading

- LAMP stack on EC2: `https://docs.aws.amazon.com/AWSCloudFormation/latest/UserGuide/deploying.applications.html#deployment-walkthrough-basic-server`

- Best practices for deploying applications on CloudFormation stacks: `https://aws.amazon.com/blogs/devops/best-practices-for-deploying-applications-on-aws-cloudformation-stacks/`

Section 3: Extending CloudFormation

CloudFormation has its limits. In this final section, we will teach it to do more than just provision resources in AWS. We will start with Custom Resources and Template Macros, as our first step in CloudFormation customization. Once we're done with this, we will briefly touch on its possible successor, AWS CDK, and a new way of provisioning serverless applications called SAM.

This section comprises the following chapters:

7
Creating Resources outside AWS Using Custom Resources

CloudFormation is usually the first infrastructure-as-code instrument to start supporting new AWS services; however, sometimes we need to communicate to services that don't support CloudFormation. Sometimes we even need to create resources outside of AWS.

CloudFormation recently started supporting external resource providers. Similar to Terraform's providers, you can develop your own provider to manage infrastructure for different cloud and manager service providers.

Since this is a brand new feature (released in November 2019), it's going to take a while for it to mature.

In this chapter, we will create external resources using custom resources—an easy way to create your own resources outside of AWS.

We will learn what they are and what their use cases are, and program our very first custom resource using AWS Lambda.

In this chapter, we will cover the following topics:

- Understanding custom resources
- The internals of the underlying Lambda function
- Writing and managing your own custom resources
- Handling the updates, deletions, and failures of custom resources

Technical requirements

The code used in this chapter can be found in the book's GitHub repository at: `https://github.com/PacktPublishing/Mastering-AWS-CloudFormation/tree/master/Chapter7`

Check out the following video to see the Code in Action:

`https://bit.ly/3bTWq4q`

Understanding custom resources

When we declare a resource in a CloudFormation template, we provide a `Type` attribute. This attribute declares a service and a resource that is going to be created—this means that CloudFormation *understands* where to go, what to do, and which API calls to make. The `AWS` is a main namespace (for example, provider), and what comes after `AWS` is another namespace, declaring the service. If it's `EC2`, then CloudFormation will send calls to EC2's API. If it's `RDS`, then it sends calls to RDS's API. The last block is the actual resource we want to create.

Custom resources (**CRs**) are the resources that don't fall under the official support of CloudFormation. These can be external providers, internal or self-hosted systems, or even services that don't support CloudFormation yet. The creation of CRs is usually a contract with three counteragents—the template developer, CR provider, and CloudFormation. While the template developer is responsible for resource declaration and the CR provider needs to develop a handler, CloudFormation acts as a broker explicitly declaring the way that both parties will communicate when a resource is created, updated, or deleted.

CRs can be declared in a long (`AWS::CloudFormation::CustomResource`) or short form (`Custom::MyResourceName`). Nonetheless, during stack operations, CloudFormation will send a specific payload to the endpoint, which we define in the resource properties.

The declaration of a CR contains the type and the properties, which will form a payload. For example, let's say we declare a CR as shown in the following code:

```
Cr:
  Type: Custom::MyResource
  Properties:
    ServiceToken: "..."
    Key1: Value1
    Key2:
      - list_element1
      - list_element2
```

CloudFormation will generate the following payload:

```
{
    "RequestType":"Create/Update/Delete",
    "ResponseURL":"http://...",
    "StackId":"...",
    "RequestId":"uniqueId for this request",
    "ResourceType":"Custom::MyResource",
    "LogicalResourceId":"Cr",
    "ResourceProperties":{
      "Key1":"Value1",
      "Key2":[
         "list_element1",
         "list_element2"
      ]
    }
}
```

This payload is then sent to the endpoint. It contains fields from the resource declaration, the stack ID, the request type (`Create` resource, `Update` resource, or `Delete` resource), and the URL to which the Lambda function must send the response object.

There are two endpoints that can receive this kind of payload: AWS Lambda and SNS.

SNS is mostly used to program the provisioning logic processed by the backend running on EC2, ECS, or even on-premise. This is not the most efficient way to provision or process CR logic, since the backend will have to be subscribed to SNS topic and run 24/7, but SNS-backed CRs increase the variety of provisioners.

In most cases, AWS engineers prefer using Lambda because of its cost efficiency, simplicity, and ease of management; however, we must always remember Lambda's limits and capabilities.

In this chapter, we will focus on developing CRs backed by AWS Lambda.

The internals of the underlying Lambda function

Lambda function is a code that is triggered by an event. Once run, it receives `event` and `context` objects and runs internal code that will process these objects.

While the `context` is just metadata of the Lambda function's execution and can be used for self-maintenance and graceful shutdown, the `event` object contains the payload that we want to focus on.

In the case of CRs, we will need to parse the stack's information, run our logic, and respond to CloudFormation. The response should contain the following fields:

- Status (either success or failed)
- Physical resource ID (since it is custom, we need to come up with our own resource ID)
- Stack ID (the same as from the CR request)
- Request ID (the same as from the CR request)
- Logical resource ID (the same as from the CR request)
- Data (may or may not be unnecessary, used for the intrinsic `Fn::GetAtt` function)
- After processing and running provisioning, the CR function must send a response to the `ResponseURL` from the original request. This response must be in the JSON format (even if the template was written in YAML).
- In the case of a successful execution, the response would be like the following:

```
{
    "Status":"SUCCESS",
    "RequestId":"...",
    "LogicalResourceId":"...",
    "StackId":"...",
    "PhysicalResourceId":"MyResourceUniqueId1234",
```

```
    "Data":{
        "Attr1":"foo",
        "Attr2":"bar"
    }
}
```

In the case of a failure, we don't need to provide Data, but we want to provide a Status and Reason, so our response object will be different:

```
{
    "Status":"FAILED",
    "Reason":"This failed because of reasons",
    "RequestId":"...",
    "LogicalResourceId":"...",
    "StackId":"...",
    "PhysicalResourceId":"MyResourceUniqueId1234"
}
```

The Reason is what we will then see in the Events section on the CloudFormation console, so it is wise to provide explanatory reasons as to why the resource failed to create.

Let's take a quick look at the flow of Lambda-backed CR:

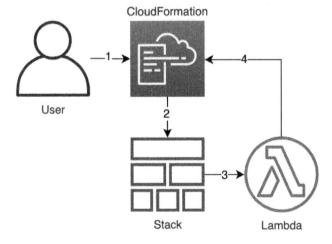

Figure 7.1 – CR flow

The preceding diagram is explained in the following steps:

1. The user runs a stack operation. At this point, CloudFormation will run a stack operation that can be creation of the stack, its update, or deletion.

2. The stack operation affects a custom resource. CloudFormation generates a payload containing the stack's and resource's metadata.

3. CloudFormation invokes the lambda function, providing it with a payload.

4. The Lambda function runs provisioning logic and returns the response to CloudFormation.

Another thing that we want to know about is the cfn-response module.

cfn-response is a wrapper that generates a response object and sends it back to CloudFormation. This module already contains the necessary attributes and methods and makes responding to CloudFormation way easier.

For example, the pseudocode using cfn-response would look like the following:

```
import cfnresponse
def handler(event, context):
    in = event['ResourceProperties']['foo']
    # do some magic
    out = generate_id(event['ResourceType'])
    cfnresponse.send(event,
                context,
                cfnresponse.SUCCESS,
                "",
                physicalResourceId=out
```

In the preceding code, we parse the event, run custom provisioning logic, and send the response to CloudFormation.

The cfn-response already has the necessary functionality, so we only need to focus on provisioning logic.

> **Important note**
>
> The cfn-response can only be imported if you upload the lambda code using ZipFile. If you use S3 for sources, you will have to program the logic on your own. The source code of cfn-response is available in AWS's documentation at https://docs.aws.amazon.com/AWSCloudFormation/latest/UserGuide/cfn-lambda-function-code-cfnresponsemodule.html#w2ab1c20c25c14b9c15.

All this theory makes no sense without practice. Let's get some hands-on experience!

Writing and managing your own custom resource

Let's start with a simple task. Let's say that we have a *shared* RDS instance and we need to create databases in it. Since CloudFormation doesn't support that out of the box, we will have to develop our CR.

Creating databases in RDS using CRs

We are going to create a CR that will connect to the RDS instance and perform SQL operations on it to create a database, user, password, and necessary privileges in the following steps:

1. Let's define our custom resource:

customdb.yaml

```yaml
CustomDb:
  Type: Custom::DB
  Properties:
    ServiceToken: # ARN of Lambda-backed CR
    DBName: # the name of our DB
    DBUser: # the username for our DB
    DBPassword: # the password for our DB's user
    RDSEndpoint: # the endpoint of RDS instance
    RDSUser: # the admin user which will access RDS DB
    RDSPassword: # the password of admin user
```

These fields should be enough to start with. Some of the properties have to be required (RDS endpoint, user, password, database name, and so on), but we will have to develop this logic in Lambda.

2.   Let's start with a skeleton:

customdb.py

```
import cfnresponse


def handler(event, context):
    physicalResourceId = ""
    cfnresponse.send(event,
                     context,
                     cfnresponse.SUCCESS,

physicalResourceId=physicalResourceId,
                     responseData="")
```

With this code, we configure the parameters that we want to make mandatory so that the process fails if one of them is not provided.

3.   Let's create a simple filter check to *fail* Lambda if some of the properties are missing:

customdb.py

```
def handler(event, context):
    # ...
    input_props = event['ResourceProperties']
    required_props = ["DBName", "RDSEndpoint", "RDSUser",
"RDSPassword"]
    missing_props = [prop for prop in required_props if
prop not in input_props]
    if missing_props:
        print(f"Required properties are missing:
{missing_props}")
        cfnresponse.send(event,
                         context,
                         cfnresponse.FAILED,
```

```
                            physicalResourceId="",
                            responseData="")
        sys.exit(1)
    # ...
```

Error handling is done at this stage. We check the keys of the event object while adding missing properties to the error message. The `cfn-response` doesn't support adding the status reason out of the box. Instead, it instructs the program to look at the CloudWatch logs, so we send our error message to `stdout`.

4. Now we need to start developing our provisioning logic. Our flow will consist of the following:

(a) Connection to the RDS instance

(b) Creation of the user

(c) Creation of the database

(d) Granting privileges to the created user on the new database.

But what if the user doesn't provide credentials for the new database? We didn't make these properties mandatory, but Lambda won't be able to create an empty user and password. We could enforce these properties, but instead we will assign them to the value of `DBName`. We also need to assign the values of other properties:

customdb.py

```
def handler(event, context):
    # ...
    db_name = input_props['DBName']
    rds_endpoint = input_props['RDSEndpoint']
    rds_user = input_props['RDSUser']
    rds_password = input_props['RDSPassword']
    if not "DBUser" in input_props or len(input_
props['DBUser']) == 0:
        db_user = db_name
    else:
        db_user = input_props['DBUser']
    if not "DBPassword" in input_props or len(input_
props['DBPassword']) == 0:
        db_password = db_name
```

```
        else:
            db_password = input_props['DBPassword']
    # ...
```

Here, we check whether the property exists and is not empty and store the value.

5.   Now we need to develop our provisioning logic. To keep the handler clean, let's
     create a separate function to clean it:

customdb.py

```python
import pymysql


def create_db(dbname, dbuser, dbpassword, rdsendpoint,
rdsuser, rdspassword):
    create_db_query = f"CREATE DATABASE {dbname};"
    create_user_query = f"CREATE USER '{dbuser}'@'%'
IDENTIFIED BY '{dbpassword}';"
    grant_query = f"GRANT ALL PRIVILEGES ON {dbname}.* TO
{dbuser}@'%'; FLUSH PRIVILEGES;"
    try:
        conn = pymysql.connect(host=rdsendpoint,
                               user=rdsuser,
                               password=rdspassword)
        cursor = conn.cursor()
        cursor.execute(create_db_query)
        cursor.execute(create_user_query)
        # ...
    except Exception as err:
        return err
    return None
```

This function (create_db()) connects to the database, runs queries, and returns
the error message if, for some reason, the creation has failed.

6. Let's call this function in our handler:

customdb.py

```python
def handler(event, context):
    # ...
    err = create_db(db_name, db_user, db_password, rds_
endpoint, rds_user, rds_password)
    if err:
        print(err)
        send(event, context, FAILED,
physicalResourceId="", responseData={})
        sys.exit(1)
    # ...
```

All good, right?

However, there is a potential problem in our Lambda. We introduced *PyMySQL*, a pure Python MySQL client (this client doesn't require external MySQL libraries to be installed, so it's a perfect module for Lambda), which is an external package and has to be installed using `pip`. If we install an external dependency, we have to package our source code and upload it to S3. If we upload it to S3, we can't import the `cfn-response` (remember the preceding note?).

7. In order to solve this, we will have to copy the code of `cfn-response` from the CloudFormation documentation (`https://docs.aws.amazon.com/AWSCloudFormation/latest/UserGuide/cfn-lambda-function-code-cfnresponsemodule.html#w2ab1c20c25c14b9c15`). So, our code will look a bit different:

customdb.py

```python
import requests
import json
import pymysql


SUCCESS = "SUCCESS"
FAILED = "FAILED"

```

```
def create_db(#...):
    # ...


def handler(event, context):
    # ...


# And the "send" function from cfn-response module...
def send(#...):
    # ...
```

8. We will introduce an improvement for the `cfn-response.send` function in the next section. For now, let's create our CR function (you might have to come up with your S3 bucket name):

```
$ aws s3 mb s3://masteringcloudformation
$ pip3 install -t custom-db/ -r custom-db/requirements.
txt
$ cd custom-db && zip -r lambda-cr.zip *
$ aws s3 cp lambda-cr.zip s3://masteringcloudformation
$ cd .. && aws cloudformation deploy \
                            --stack-name cr \
                            --template-file cr.yaml \
                            --capabilities CAPABILITY_
IAM
```

9. Now we need to deploy our stack with an RDS instance (MySQL). Replace `$VPCID` with the ID of the VPC you have in your account:

```
$ aws cloudformation deploy --stack-name rds \
                            --template-file rds.yaml \
                            --parameter-overrides \
                            VpcId=$VPCID
```

10. Once this is done, we can deploy our CR stack:

```
aws cloudformation deploy --stack-name customdb \
                            --template-file customdb.yaml
```

11. Once the resource is created, we can evaluate the created database by connecting to it:

```
$ mysql -u mydbuser -pfoobar1234 -h $RDS_INSTANCE mydb
```

And that's it! Our CR function is capable of creating the new resource; however, it is far from perfect and will definitely fail when we want to update or delete this resource from CloudFormation's state.

In the next section, we will focus on how to manage updates and deletions and how to work with stack operation errors.

Handling updates, deletions, and failures of CRs

Our CR can create a database for us. But try to guess what will happen if you attempt to delete this resource or stack from CloudFormation.

It will fail to delete. Why? Because our CR function runs only one function, `create_db`, it doesn't matter which *request type* is received by CloudFormation. Exactly the same will happen if we try to update our database.

We need to add support for *updates* and *deletes* for our Lambda. We will start with the delete functionality, because what we will do is make our custom resource immutable.

This means that whenever we change our custom database, the old one will always be deleted. Sounds scary? Don't worry: unfortunately, this is the default behavior for custom resources. Moreover, some AWS resources are also *replaced* (for example, a new resource is created while the old one is being deleted), even if nothing major is being changed.

Deleting resource

We will cover the delete operation in the following steps:

1. We will create an extra function in our Lambda script and call it `delete_db`:

customdb.py

```
def delete_db(dbname, dbuser, rdsendpoint, rdsuser,
rdspassword):
    return None
```

We have the skeleton of our function. It has arguments similar to `create_db`, except `dbpassword`; we don't need to know the user's password to delete it from the database.

2. Now let's add the actual deletion logic. First, we need the queries to run on the database:

customdb.py

```python
def delete_db(dbname, dbuser, rdsendpoint, rdsuser,
rdspassword):
    delete_db_query = f"DROP DATABASE {dbname}"
    delete_user_query = f"DROP USER '{dbuser}'"
    return None
```

3. Next, we need the `try-except` block with a database connection and query execution:

customdb.py

```python
def delete_db(dbname, dbuser, rdsendpoint, rdsuser,
rdspassword):
    delete_db_query = f"DROP DATABASE {dbname}"
    delete_user_query = f"DROP USER '{dbuser}'"
    try:
        conn = pymysql.connect(host=rdsendpoint,
                               user=rdsuser,
                               password=rdspassword)
        cursor = conn.cursor()
        cursor.execute(delete_db_query)
        cursor.execute(delete_user_query)
        cursor.close()
        conn.commit()
        conn.close()
    except Exception as err:
        return err
    return None
```

What we do here is connect to the same RDS, run queries, and close the connection. If anything goes wrong, we return error. If not, we return `None` (an empty Python object).

4. Now we need to parse the incoming event and obtain the request type. We will do this in the `handler` function:

customdb.py

```
import ...
# ...
def handler(event, context):
# ...
    if event['RequestType'] == "Delete":
        err = delete_db(db_name, db_user, rds_endpoint,
rds_user, rds_password)
    elif event['RequestType'] == "Create":
        err = create_db(db_name, db_user, db_password,
rds_endpoint, rds_user, rds_password)
# ...
```

What we've changed is the actual function that runs during the stack operation. If CloudFormation sends a `Delete` request, then we go to the RDS instance and drop the database and user. If it sends `Create`, then we create a database.

5. We need to update the source code. Since we already have all the stacks in place, let's do it manually:

```
$ cd custom-db/
$ zip -r lambda-cr.zip *
$ aws s3 cp lambda-cr.zip s3://masteringcloudformation
--profile personal
$ aws cloudformation list-stack-resources --stack-name cr
| jq .StackResourceSummaries[0].PhysicalResourceId
"cr-CrFunction-EX3NB14PJARD"
$ aws lambda update-function-code --function-
name cr-CrFunction-EX3NB14PJARD --s3-bucket
masteringcloudformation --s3-key lambda-cr.zip
# long output from Lambda...
```

6. Now let's delete the stack:

```
$ aws cloudformation delete-stack --stack-name customdb
$ aws cloudformation list-stacks \
                    --stack-status-filter DELETE_
COMPLETE
{
    "StackSummaries": [
      # ....
        {
            # ...
            "StackName": "customdb",
            # ...
            "StackStatus": "DELETE_COMPLETE",
            # ...
        },
  # ...
}
```

7. Now let's check that the database really doesn't exist:

```
$ mysql -u rdsuser -pbarfoo12344321 -h $RDSENDPOINT
mysql > show databases;
+--------------------+
| Database           |
+--------------------+
| information_schema |
| innodb             |
| mysql              |
| performance_schema |
| sys                |
+--------------------+
5 rows in set (0.02 sec)
```

This confirms that the Delete operation works as expected.

Let's add support for updates so that we can change databases, users, and so on within our CR.

Updating resources

Our resource is immutable. If it's changed, then the old one is deleted and the new one is created. CloudFormation sends an Update request to create a new resource. Once it is done, during UPDATE_COMPLETE_CLEANUP_IN_PROGRESS CloudFormation will send a Delete request with the properties of the resource that was created during the previous stack operation:

1. Since we already support create and delete operations, all we need to do is to change the filtering to support both Create and Update in the handler function:

customdb.py

```python
import ...
# ...
def handler(event, context):
# ...
    if event['RequestType'] == "Delete":
        err = delete_db(db_name, db_user, rds_endpoint,
rds_user, rds_password)
    elif event['RequestType'] in ["Create", "Update"]:
        err = create_db(db_name, db_user, db_password,
rds_endpoint, rds_user, rds_password)
# ...
```

2. We are going to repackage our function, upload it to S3, and update the Lambda function's code (the same way we did in the previous section). Since we deleted the custom database stack, we need to recreate and then update it:

```
$ aws cloudformation deploy --stack-name customdb \
                            --template-file customdb.yaml
$ aws cloudformation deploy --stack-name customdb \
                            --template-file customdb.yaml
\
                            --parameter-overrides \
                            DBName=mynewdb \
                            DBUser=mynewuser
```

3. When the deployment is finished, we can check the database again:

```
$ mysql -u rdsuser -pbarfoo12344321 -h $RDSENDPOINT
mysql> show databases;
+--------------------+
| Database           |
+--------------------+
| information_schema |
| innodb             |
| mysql              |
| mynewdb            |
| performance_schema |
| sys                |
+--------------------+
6 rows in set (0.02 sec)
```

All good! Our custom resource now fully supports creation, updating, and deletion!
Now we are going to teach our CR function a few more tricks.

Extra features for the custom database function

Our CR performs as expected, but there is always room for improvement. In this section,
we will make our CR nicer and more self-explanatory in case of failures.

Custom status reasons

Until now, if we had an error, it was returned as an invitation to read the Lambda logs.
This is because cfn-response.send has the following line:

```
responseBody['Reason'] = 'See the details in CloudWatch Log
Stream: ' + context.log_stream_name
```

This Reason string is sent to CloudFormation and is mandatory when the Status is
FAILED. The preceding string generation is hardcoded into cfn-response; however,
since we copied the code, we have a control on it.

We are going to add support for custom status reasons by going through the following steps:

1. Let's make a few changes to the send() function:

customdb.py

```python
def send(event, context, responseStatus, responseData,
responseReason="", physicalResourceId=None,
noEcho=False):
# ...
    responseBody = {}
    responseBody['Status'] = responseStatus
    responseBody['Reason'] = responseReason
# ...
```

Here, we add the non-mandatory responseReason argument and use it as a value for responseBody['Reason']. This will give us the ability to send our own custom messages to CloudFormation.

2. Now we are going to make our provisional logic send these reasons. Let's start with our required properties check:

customdb.py

```python
# ...
def handler(event, context):
    input_props = event['ResourceProperties']
    required_props = ["DBName", "RDSEndpoint", "RDSUser",
"RDSPassword"]
    missing_props = [prop for prop in required_props if
prop not in input_props]
    if missing_props:
        reason = f"Required properties are missing:
{missing_props}"
        send(event, context, FAILED,
responseReason=reason, responseData={})
        sys.exit(1)
# ...
```

3.   Let's check this error handling by creating a stack with one of the missing properties (*don't forget to update the function code!*):

```
aws cloudformation deploy \
    --stack-name broken-custom \
    --template-file customdb_missing_property.yaml
```

We will see some very interesting behavior:

Logical ID	Status	Status reason
customdb -broken	⊗ ROLLBACK_FAILED	The following resource(s) failed to delete: [CustomDb].
CustomDb	⊗ DELETE_FAILED	Failed to delete resource. Required properties are missing: ['DBName']
CustomDb	ⓘ DELETE_IN_PROGRESS	-
customdb -broken	⊗ ROLLBACK_IN_PROGRESS	The following resource(s) failed to create: [CustomDb]. . Rollback requested by user.
CustomDb	⊗ CREATE_FAILED	Failed to create resource. Required properties are missing: ['DBName']
CustomDb	ⓘ CREATE_IN_PROGRESS	Resource creation Initiated
CustomDb	ⓘ CREATE_IN_PROGRESS	-

Figure 7.2 – CloudFormation console

This is because our check is applied to any request type. When creation fails, CloudFormation still considers the resource to be created and wants to clean it up. The database doesn't exist, so CloudFormation will get stuck in a loop until at some point it will give up and say DELETE_FAILED.

In order to make our Custom Resource more error free, we need to apply few changes to the Lambda function.

Sending a success upon the deletion of nothing

CloudFormation insists there is a resource. We know there isn't. If we try to delete a database or user that doesn't exist, our script will definitely fail, and so will the stack operation in CloudFormation.

To make our CR more redundant, we will make our CR function able to handle
this properly:

1. Let's add a few lines to our function, where we check if there are some
    properties missing:

customdb.py

```
def handler(event, context):
# ...
    if missing_props:
        if event['RequestType'] == "Delete":
            send(event, context, SUCCESS,
responseData={})
            sys.exit(0)
        reason = f"Required properties are missing:
{missing_props}"
        send(event, context, FAILED,
responseReason=reason, responseData={})
        sys.exit(1)
# ...
```

Here, we check whether CloudFormation is performing deletion. If it is and no
props are provided, then that means it is a dry cleanup. All we need to do is to
report to CloudFormation that everything was successful.

2. We'll upload the new code and rerun stack creation:

```
$ aws cloudformation delete-stack --stack-name broken-
custom
$ aws cloudformation deploy \
    --stack-name broken-custom \
    --template-file customdb_missing_property.yaml
```

The result will be different this time:

Logical ID	Status	Status reason
customdb-broken	⊗ ROLLBACK_COMPLETE	-
CustomDb	⊘ DELETE_COMPLETE	-
CustomDb	ⓘ DELETE_IN_PROGRESS	-
customdb-broken	⊗ ROLLBACK_IN_PROGRESS	The following resource(s) failed to create: [CustomDb]. . Rollback requested by user.
CustomDb	⊗ CREATE_FAILED	Failed to create resource. Required properties are missing: ['DBName']

Figure 7.3 – CloudFormation console

But there is one more thing that we want to add. What if the database that is to be deleted doesn't exist anymore (for example, it was deleted manually)?

3.   Let's also handle that eventuality by setting up the following code:

customdb.py

```
def delete_db(dbname, dbuser, rdsendpoint, rdsuser,
rdspassword):
# ...
    db_exists_query = f"SHOW DATABASES LIKE '{dbname}'"
    user_exists_query = f"SELECT user FROM mysql.user
where user='{dbuser}'"
    try:
        # ...
        db_exists = cursor.execute(db_exists_query)
        if db_exists:
            cursor.execute(delete_db_query)
        user_exists = cursor.execute(user_exists_query)
        if user_exists:
            cursor.execute(delete_user_query)
    # ...
    except Exception as err:
        return err
    return None
```

What we do is we check whether both the database and user exist in the database. If not, we skip the deletion query to avoid getting `database doesn't exist` or `Operation DROP USER failed for` errors.

That being said, we've added custom status reasons to our CR function and made it more error resistant.

Summary

In this chapter, we learned about custom resources, the most universal way to extend CloudFormation. We created our own CR backed by AWS Lambda, made it stable and secure, and also made it able to handle updates, deletions, and errors.

Custom resources are widely used to either create resources in AWS that are not yet supported by CloudFormation or create resources outside of AWS, whether they are other cloud platforms or your own platforms and systems running on EC2.

We covered custom resources and provisioning logic and understood what actually happens under the hood. To get a real hands-on experience with CRs, we developed our own CR, made it error resistant, and added support for custom reason messages.

In the next chapter we will learn about another extension of CloudFormation called the template macro. Stay tuned!

Questions

1. What are the possible request types for CRs?
2. Is it possible to use `cfnresponse` if we package the Lambda function with external dependencies?
3. Which AWS services are used for CR processing?
4. Which CR response object has to be used to specify the reason of failed resource changes?
5. What are the `event` and `context` in Lambda?

Further reading

- Alex DeBrie's blog on custom resources: `https://www.alexdebrie.com/posts/cloudformation-custom-resources/`
- GitHub repository with sample custom resources: `https://github.com/aws-samples/aws-cfn-custom-resource-examples`

8
Dynamically Rendering the Template Using Template Macros

Sometimes when we work with templates, we want to dynamically assign values to resources or alter the template quickly during stack operations.

One of the most well-known template macros is **SAM** or the **Serverless Application Model**, which is a simplified CloudFormation template for serverless applications (we will cover SAM in the next few chapters). Another well-known macro is `AWS::Include`, which allows us to append the CloudFormation template with boilerplate snippets.

In this chapter, we will learn about template macros and their use cases, and we will develop our own macros.

In this chapter, we will cover the following topics:

- Understanding use cases of template macros
- Introducing the template macro
- Writing your own macros

Technical requirements

The code used in this chapter can be found in the book's GitHub repository at `https://github.com/PacktPublishing/Mastering-AWS-CloudFormation/tree/master/Chapter8`.

Check out the following video to see the Code in Action:

`https://bit.ly/2zBBLnd`

Understanding the use cases of the template macro

Before we dive into the internals of macros, we need to know what we can solve with them. Let's look at a few cases and examples.

Auto filling resource property values

Imagine having a launch template where you need to define an AMI ID. For Amazon Linux AMI, you could use AWS's parameter store:

```
Parameters:
  ImageId:
    Type: AWS::SSM::Parameter::Value<AWS::EC2::Image::Id>
    Default: '/aws/service/ami-amazon-linux-latest/amzn2-ami-
hvm-x86_64-gp2'
Resources:
  LaunchTemplate:
    Type: "AWS::EC2::LaunchTemplate"
    Properties:
      LaunchTemplateData:
        ImageId: !Ref ImageId
```

But what if we don't use Amazon Linux, but Ubuntu? We'd have to manually specify the AMI IDs and use mappings:

```
Mappings:
  RegionMap:
    us-east-1:
      "HVM64": "ami-123"
    us-west-1:
      "HVM64": "ami-456"
    # and so on...
Resources:
  Inst:
    Type: AWS::EC2::Instance
    Properties:
      ImageId: !FindInMap [RegionMap, !Ref "AWS::Region",
HVM64]
```

Or we can build a macro that looks it up for us and use it in our template.

The following template is an example of how to fill an AMI ID using a macro:

```
Resources:
  LaunchTemplate:
    Type: "AWS::EC2::LaunchTemplate"
    Properties:
      LaunchTemplateData:
        ImageId:
          Fn::Transform:
            Name: FindAmi
            Parameters:
              OSFamily: ubuntu
```

As you can see in the preceding example, the macro name is supplied after the intrinsic function, Fn::Transform, followed by its parameters. During the stack operation, the macro will store the necessary AMI ID. Let's look at another example.

Adding extra resources

Let's say we have some sort of resource that is the same for every stack, but has to be the part of each one individually—for example, CloudWatch rules and alerts for applications. We could copy-paste the same resource declaration over and over again, which is considered to be a code duplication and is bad practice.

For cases like this, there is a CloudFormation macro called `AWS::Include`. The `AWS::Include` macro looks for a template on S3 and appends the current template with an extra one. The `AWS::Include` macro is not a *global* macro, so it has to be declared in the `Resources` section, as shown in the following code:

```
Resources:
  # ... some of our resources...
  "Fn::Transform":
    Name: "AWS::Include"
    Parameters:
      Location: "s3://mybucket/my_set_of_resources.yaml"
```

Although it is a common macro, we should avoid using duplicated resources and organize our stack properly.

Making resource declaration easier for developers

We have a standard way of developing applications. Let's say that each application is an ECS task running on Fargate. It may or may not have additional resources and it will always run on the same ECS cluster as the others. We could make a huge template with conditional elements and ask developers to provide a lot of parameters or we can make a nice and easy-to-use template for them with the help of a macro.

The following example template shows how this *standard* application will look:

```
Transform: StandardApplication
Resources:
  Application:
    Properties:
      TaskCount: 1
      Memory: 512
      CPU: 256
      RDS: postgresql
      RDSSize: db.t2.micro
      # and so on...
```

During transformation, the macro will evaluate the properties and render a new template, such as the following:

```
Resources:
  EcsTaskDefinition:
    Type: # ...
    Properties:
      Cpu: 256
      Memory: 512
      # ...
  EcsService:
    Type: #...
    Propeties:
      DesiredCount: 1
      # ...
# and so on...
```

Developers will always have control over their application's infrastructure and resources, yet will not have to dive deep into CloudFormation and AWS.

This all sounds good, but how do we make this happen? Let's look at what exactly a template macro is.

Introducing the template macro

First of all, macros are an optional part of CloudFormation. AWS already provides us with its own macros (`AWS::Serverless` and `AWS::Include`)—they are a part of CloudFormation and are executed whenever we use a transform in a template or resource.

Custom macros (that is, macros created by us) are also part of the CloudFormation and are created as a resource with a `AWS::CloudFormation::Macro` type. Each macro in particular is a Lambda function, which is similar to a custom resource, as it receives an event from CloudFormation and needs to return a response.

This Lambda function will receive a part of the template (or the full template), run custom processing, and return a transformed template.

The request from CloudFormation will look like the following:

```
{
    "region" : "...",
    "accountId" : "...",
    "fragment" : { ... },
    "transformId" : "...",
    "params" : { ... },
    "requestId" : "...",
    "templateParameterValues" : { ... }
}
```

Here are the key code terms and their description:

- fragment: Either a part or the full template
- params: A list of parameters, if the macro function is invoked using the intrinsic function Fn::Transform
- templateParameterValues: Template parameters

templateParameterValues, unlike params, these values are evaluated before processing (during the template validation step).

After processing, our Lambda should return a response. This response should contain a request identifier (exactly the same as in the original request), status, and processed content. All in all, it will look like the following:

```
{
    "requestId" : "...",
    "status" : "...",
    "fragment" : { ... }
}
```

Before we create our own macro, we need to know about a few limitations that we might face.

Considerations

Macros bring plenty of benefits for easing the development of CloudFormation templates, but there are many things that we need to keep in mind when writing them.

Mainly, we need to know the following facts:

- Macros will only work in the regions where AWS Lambda is available
- Processed templates must pass the validation check
- Macros don't support iteration—we can't include a macro in a macro
- Macros don't support `Fn::ImportValue`
- Macros are not supported in `StackSets`

> **Important note**
> For the full list of considerations, please read CloudFormation's documentation (`https://docs.aws.amazon.com/AWSCloudFormation/latest/UserGuide/template-macros.html`).

These are the main things that we need to bear in mind. Now, let's build macros for a few of the cases that were mentioned in the beginning of this chapter.

Writing your own macro

In this section, we are going to develop macros to solve the cases introduced in the first section of this chapter, the *Understanding the use cases of template macros section*. This will help us to get some hands-on experience and practice partial and full template processing.

Let's start with the AMI ID filler!

AMI ID filler

Let's start with a simple task and create a macro that will automatically find the AMI ID for EC2. By the end of this section, we will have a macro that automatically puts a correct AMI in the resource properties.

As you might remember, our main template will look like the following:

```
Resources:
  LaunchTemplate:
    Type: "AWS::EC2::LaunchTemplate"
    Properties:
      LaunchTemplateData:
        # This is a replacement for the field ImageId:
        Fn::Transform:
```

```
        Name: AMIFiller
        Parameters:
            OSFamily: ubuntu
```

This means that CloudFormation will send the request with the following payload:

```
{
    "region" : "...", # region name, where the stack is
    "accountId" : "...",  # AWS account ID
    "fragment" : { ... }, # the fragment of the template
    "transformId" : "...", # unique ID of transformation
    "params" : { "OSFamily": "ubuntu" },
    "requestId" : "...", # request ID for Lambda
    "templateParameterValues" : { ... } # template parameters
}
```

So all we need to do is return the string that contains the AMI ID that we need. The response body would look like the following:

```
{
    "requestId" : "...", # same as in original request
    "status" : "...",  # SUCCESS or FAILURE
    "fragment" : { "ImageId": "ami-123454321" }
}
```

Let's begin by developing a Lambda function so that our macro can find a proper AMI:

1. We will start with an actual function that will invoke EC2's API in order to retrieve the AMI ID:

amifinder.py

```
image_names = {
    "amazonlinux2": "amzn2-ami-hvm-2.0.20191217.0-
x86_64-gp2",
    "ubuntu": "ubuntu/images/hvm-ssd/ubuntu-bionic-18.04-
amd64-server-20200112",
    "rhel": "RHEL-8.0.0_HVM-20190618-x86_64-1-
Hourly2-GP2",
```

```
        "sles": "suse-sles-15-sp1-v20191112-hvm-ssd-x86_64"
    }


def get_image(img_name):
    client = boto3.client("ec2")
    resp = client.describe_images(Filters=[{"Name":
"name",
                                            "Values": [img_
name]}])
    return resp['Images'][0]['ImageId']
```

Since AWS has plenty of AMIs (both new and older versions), it is hard to find the necessary image with a single word (like `"ubuntu"` or `"rhel"`), so we will create a dictionary that will contain the exact AMI name.

Then we use a function that will connect to the API and request the AMI ID for that name.

2. Now we need our handler function:

amifinder.py

```
def lambda_handler(event, context):
    response = {}
    response['requestId'] = event['requestId']
    response['fragment'] = {"ImageId": ""}
    response['status'] = "SUCCESS"
    osfamily = event['params']['OSFamily']

    if osfamily not in image_names.keys():
        response['status'] = "FAILURE"
        return response

    image_id = get_image(image_names[osfamily])
    response['fragment']["ImageId"] = image_id
    return response
```

This function will parse the event from CloudFormation. If the supplied parameter `OSFamily` doesn't equal `ubuntu`, `amazonlinux2`, `rhel`, or `sles`, it will immediately return `FAILURE` with an empty body, signaling to CloudFormation that the macro has failed; otherwise, it will invoke the `get_image()` function and form a proper response.

3. Now we need to create a macro stack (thereby registering the macro function):

```
$ aws cloudformation deploy --stack-name amimacro \
                    --template-file macro.yaml \
                    --capabilities CAPABILITY_IAM
```

4. Our macro is in place. Let's create a template to test it out. Our testing template is small and simple; all we need is to check that the macro performs its function:

lt.yaml

```
Resources:
  Lt:
    Type: AWS::EC2::LaunchTemplate
    Properties:
      LaunchTemplateData:
        Fn::Transform:
          Name: AMIFiller
          Parameters:
            OSFamily: "ubuntu"
```

5. We are going to create a stack from this template:

```
$ aws cloudformation deploy --stack-name lt \
                    --template-file lt.yaml
```

6. After a while, we will see our stack created. Let's check the template on the CloudFormation console:

Template

⬤ View processed template

```
AWSTemplateFormatVersion: "2010-09-09"
Resources:
  Lt:
    Type: AWS::EC2::LaunchTemplate
    Properties:
      LaunchTemplateData:
        Fn::Transform:
          Name: AMIFiller
          Parameters:
            OSFamily: "ubuntu"
```

Figure 8.1 – CloudFormation console – unprocessed template

There is an interesting trigger. Let's click on it and see what happens!

Template

◐ View processed template

```
{
  "AWSTemplateFormatVersion": "2010-09-09",
  "Resources": {
    "Lt": {
      "Properties": {
        "LaunchTemplateData": {
          "ImageId": "ami-0b418580298265d5c"
        }
      },
      "Type": "AWS::EC2::LaunchTemplate"
    }
  }
}
```

Figure 8.2 – CloudFormation console – processed template

So what actually happened is that the macro ran a transformation changing the block where we call `Fn::Transform` to an image ID. Exactly what we wanted!

Now, let's simulate an error. We are going to change the `OSFamily` parameter from `ubuntu` to something that is not in our macro's dictionary and rerun the stack deployment:

lt.yaml

```
Resources:
  Lt:
    Type: AWS::EC2::LaunchTemplate
    Properties:
      LaunchTemplateData:
        Fn::Transform:
          Name: AMIFiller
          Parameters:
            OSFamily: "yolo"
```

7. Now let's deploy the stack:

```
$ aws cloudformation deploy --stack-name lt --template-
file lt.yaml
Waiting for changeset to be created..
Failed to create the changeset: Waiter
ChangeSetCreateComplete failed: Waiter encountered a
terminal failure state Status: FAILED. Reason: Transform
ACCT_ID::AMIFiller failed without an error message.
```

> **Important note**
>
> Note that the stack update failed *before* the execution of changeset. This is because CloudFormation runs template validation before *and* after macro processing, and since our function returned `FAILED`, CloudFormation couldn't continue.

This said, let's create a more powerful template macro that will render the whole application template from just a bunch of input data.

Rendering the application template from a short declaration

In this section, we are going to develop a macro that will create a full CloudFormation stack by transforming a shortened version of it—the *standard application* declaration.

> **Important note**
> Don't forget to check the repository for the full version of the macro!

So, we have the following kind of template for our so-called standard application:

app.yaml

```yaml
Transform: StandardApplication
Resources:
  Application:
    Properties:
      ApplicationImage: ""
      ApplicationPort: 0
      TaskCount: 0
      Memory: 0
      CPU: 0
      RDS: ""
      RDSSize: ""
      RDSMultiAz: False
      NeedsBalancer: False
      PubliclyAvailable: False
```

This application may or may not have the following resources:

- **Relational Database Service (RDS)** Instance
- **Elastic Load Balancer (ELS)**
- **Elastic Container Service (ECS)** Service

Imagine a case where the developers, who are mainly focused on solving business cases, don't care about the underlying infrastructure, so we as cloud engineers will have to take care of it. The only requirement for the developers is that they must supply a valid Docker image.

Transformation is applied to the template as a whole—this means that we need stricter and more complex processing logic. With the inputs, we will understand which resources to create and which properties to assign to them.

Let's first build our skeleton for the macro:

standard-app.py

```python
def render_ecs(input):
    ecs_definition = {}
    return ecs_definition

def render_rds(input):
    rds_definition = {}
    return rds_definition

def render_elb(input):
    elb_definition = {}
    return elb_definition

def lambda_handler(event, context):
    response = {}
    response['requestId'] = event['requestId']
    response['status'] = "SUCCESS"
    response['fragment'] = {}

    return response
```

What we do here is create three additional functions, each of which is responsible for processing the input data (for example, properties) and create the necessary resource declarations.

These functions are going to be as follows:

- render_ecs()
- render_rds()
- render_elb()

But before that, we are going to parse the incoming payload in the lambda handler function.

Parsing properties

Before we render the final template, we need to make a decision based on which resources we are going to create. We do this by parsing the input properties. According to our template, the `fragment` of CloudFormation's request will look like the following:

```
"fragment" : {
  "Resources": {
    "Application": {
      "Properties": {
        "ApplicationImage": "",
        "ApplicationPort": 0,
        "TaskCount": 0,
        "Memory": 0,
        "CPU": 0,
        "RDSEngine": "",
        "RDSSize": "",
        "RDSMultiAz": "",
        "NeedsBalancer": false,
        "PublciclyAvailable": false
      }
    }
  }
}
```

At least four of the properties are mandatory: image, network port, count, memory, and CPU; otherwise, we've got nothing to declare for our ECS task. Let's add a check in our lambda handler:

standard-app.py

```
def lambda_handler(event, context):
    # ...
    required_properties = ["ApplicationImage",
"ApplicationPort", "TaskCount", "Memory", "CPU"]
```

```
    properties = event['fragment']['Resources']['Application']
['Properties']
    for req in required_properties:
        if req not in properties.keys() or not properties[req]:
            response['status'] = "FAILED"
            return response
    # ...
```

If at least one of the properties is not set or is set to null, the lambda will respond with FAILED.

In addition to the required properties, we have optional ones. Those declare if we need additional resources (such as RDS Instance or ELB) and what their properties are.

The RDSEngine, RDSSize, and RDSMultiAz properties provide information on the RDS Instance that we will provision. If RDSEngine is not specified, we assume that no database is required. For RDSSize, we will have a default value of db.t2.micro and for RDSMultiAz, we will have false. Let's add this to our handler:

standard-app.py

```
def lambda_handler(event, context):
    # ...
    rds_props = {}
    rds_props['RDSEngine'] = ""
    rds_props['RDSSize'] = "db.t2.micro"
    rds_props['RDSMultiAz'] = "false"

    for key in rds_props.keys():
        if key in properties.keys() and properties[key]:
            rds_props[key] = properties[key]
    # ...
```

What we do here is we set the default values to RDS properties and the null value to RDSEngine. If they are provided in the CloudFormation's request, we overwrite them.

We will do the same with the ELB properties:

standard-app.py

```
def lambda_handler(event, context):
    # ...
```

```
elb_props = {}
elb_props['NeedBalancer'] = False
elb_props['PubliclyAvailable'] = False

for key in elb_props.keys():
    if key in properties.keys() and properties[key]:
        elb_props[key] = properties[key]
# ...
```

Now when we have all our properties sorted, we can start developing our provisioning logic.

Declaring resources from the macro

Since the macro must return a valid JSON template, this is the first (and hopefully the last) time that we write templates in JSON format.

We are going to improve the render_ecs() function so that it returns a valid declaration. We already know that we receive the application image, its port, CPU share settings, task count, and memory settings properties.

At the same time, we know that we need to provision CloudWatch logs, the ECS task definition, and it's service, both of which are compatible with ECS Fargate.

Let's build a skeleton for the ECS task definition. We will follow the same formatting as we did for the CloudFormation JSON template (you will find the full version on GitHub):

standard-app.py

```
def render_ecs(input):
    # ...
    ecs_task_definition = {
    # ...
        "Family": "",  # placeholder
    # ...
        "Name": "",  # placeholder
        "Image": "",  # placeholder
    # ...
        "ContainerPort": "",  # placeholder
    # ...
```

```
        "awslogs-stream-prefix": ""   # placeholder
    # ...
        "Cpu": "",   # placeholder
        "Memory": "",   # placeholder
    # ...
}
```

Our ECS task definition is now a dictionary object. We need to fill those placeholders with the values from the input:

standard-app.py

```python
def render_ecs(input):
    # ...
    application_image = input['ApplicationImage']
    application_name = application_image.strip(":")
    ecs_task_definition_properties = ecs_task_
definition['TaskDefinition']['Properties']
    ecs_task_definition_properties['Family'] = application_name
    ecs_task_definition_properties['ContainerDefinitions'][0]
['Name'] = application_name
    ecs_task_definition_properties['ContainerDefinitions'][0]
['Image'] = application_image
    # and so on...
```

Once the task definition has all the values, we can continue with the ECS and CloudWatch logs.

By the end our, function will look like the following:

standard-app.py

```python
def render_ecs(input):
    ecs_definition = {}
    ecs_task_definition = { ... }
    # generation of ecs_task_definition...
    ecs_service_definition = { ... }
    # generation of ecs_service_definition...
    ecs_definition['Logs'] = { ... }
```

```
ecs_definition['Sg'] = { ... }
# generation of the rest...
ecs_definition.update(ecs_task_definition)
ecs_definition.update(ecs_service_definition)

return ecs_definition
```

In the end, we will retrieve a set of CloudFormation resources required for our application, such as ECS task definition, service, CloudWatch logs, EC2 security groups, and so on.

The generation of additional resources (ELB and RDS Instance) is similar, so let's not focus on this one and jump to the deployment of our macro.

Deploying a standard app

By going through the following steps, we will deploy a macro and test it out:

1. Since our application needs to have a foundation (ECS cluster, network, and so on), we first need to provision those (you will find them in the repository):

```
$ aws cloudformation deploy --stack-name core \
                            --template-file core.yaml \
                            --capabilities CAPABILITY_IAM
```

2. Once it is deployed, we can provision our macro. Our code is too big to fit in a CloudFormation template, so we will have to upload it manually to S3:

```
$ aws s3 mb s3://masteringcfn # your bucket name may
differ
$ zip lambda-macro.zip standard-app.py
$ aws cloudformation deploy --stack-name standard-app-
macro \
                            --template-file macro.yaml \
                            --capabilities CAPABILITY_IAM
```

3. All set. We can proceed with our application:

```
$ aws cloudformation deploy --stack-name app \
                            --template-file app.yaml
```

4. Let's take a look at the CloudFormation console. We are interested in what our template will look like after processing:

Template

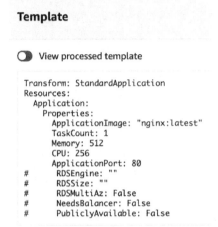

Figure 8.3 – CloudFormation console – unprocessed template

But we are interested in the processed template:

Template

○ View processed template

```
{
  "Resources": {
    "Logs": {
      "Type": "AWS::Logs::LogGroup",
      "Properties": {
        "LogGroupName": "nginx",
        "RetentionInDays": 1
      }
    },
    "Sg": {
      "Type": "AWS::EC2::SecurityGroup",
      "Properties": {
        "GroupDescription": "Security Group",
        "VpcId": {
          "Fn::ImportValue": "VpcId"
        }
      }
    },
    "TaskDefinition": {
      "Type": "AWS::ECS::TaskDefinition",
      "Properties": {
        "Family": "nginx",
        "RequiresCompatibilities": [
          "FARGATE"
        ],
        "ContainerDefinitions": [
          {
            "Name": "nginx",
            "Image": "nginx:latest",
            "PortMappings": [
              {
                "ContainerPort": 80,
                "Protocol": "tcp"
              }
```

Figure 8.4 – CloudFormation console – processed template

That's it! We have successfully created our first macro that processes the whole template! With this knowledge, we can tweak and extend the CloudFormation templates in the way that we need to.

Summary

In this chapter, we have learned about the macro, a tool that allows us to transform templates. We've learned that AWS has its own macros—`AWS::Serverless` and `AWS::Include`—and what macros consist of.

To learn about macro processing, we also developed our own macros. Now we know how and when we can use them.

Macros allow AWS engineers to avoid complexity in the templates by taking this complexity over and solving it using Lambda functions. The best example of how macros can make templates simple to write and read is the AWS **Serverless Application Model (SAM)**, and we will cover this in more detail in *Chapter 10, Deploying Serverless Applications Using AWS SAM*.

In the next chapter, we will learn about AWS—**Cloud Development Kit**. CDK introduces a completely different way of creating and managing CloudFormation stacks and allows AWS engineers to **programmatically** declare infrastructure.

See you in the next chapter!

Questions

1. When a macro processes the template, in which format is it returned?
2. What is a *fragment* in CloudFormation's transform request?
3. If the macro function is deployed in the `us-east-1` region, can we create a stack that uses it in `us-east-2`?
4. What will happen if the macro function returns a status other than `SUCCESS`?
5. Can you use multiple macros in a single template?

Further reading

- Alex DeBrie's blog on CloudFormation macros: `https://www.alexdebrie.com/posts/cloudformation-macros/`
- GitHub repository with macro examples: `https://github.com/aws-cloudformation/aws-cloudformation-macros`

9
Generating CloudFormation Templates Using AWS CDK

Now we are going to learn about one of the latest developments from AWS—**Cloud Development Kit,** or **CDK**. CDK is not meant to be a replacement for CloudFormation. Instead, it was developed to add additional functionality to CloudFormation.

CDK is a framework that supports multiple programming languages and allows AWS engineers to declare infrastructure literally as code, thereby increasing the speed of AWS development. By the end of this chapter, you will have a running infrastructure generated by CDK.

In this chapter, we will cover the following topics:

- Introducing AWS CDK
- Facilitating template development with AWS CDK
- Writing your first template using AWS CDK and Python

Technical requirements

The code used in this chapter can be found in this book's GitHub repository at `https://github.com/PacktPublishing/Mastering-AWS-CloudFormation/tree/master/Chapter9/app`.

Check out the following video to see the Code in Action:

`https://bit.ly/3aPNXxJ`

Introducing AWS CDK

CDK is not the first attempt to generate CloudFormation templates with high-level programming languages. Since writing complex CloudFormation templates can be a long-running task with many repetitive actions, developers were interested in finding a different way of generating templates.

One of those ways was a Python framework called *Troposphere*, developed by the Cloudtools team and released in 2013 (`https://github.com/cloudtools/troposphere`). Another attempt was made by AWS Labs in 2017, when they released a similar library named *GoFormation*, written in Golang (`https://github.com/awslabs/goformation`).

In the end, AWS came up with a framework that not only provided a full infrastructure-as-code experience, but also supported multiple programming languages. This framework was called AWS Cloud Development Kit, or CDK.

CDK supports the following programming languages:

- TypeScript
- JavaScript
- Python
- C#
- Java

CDK's team promises to add more languages to this list, but in the meantime, any company that is willing to integrate CDK into their development workflow should use the language that they feel most comfortable with.

CDK as a framework has a term of *constructs*, which represent the building blocks of infrastructure that need to be provisioned. These constructs can be the following:

- **CloudFormation resources**: Examples include S3 buckets, DynamoDB tables, and EC2 instances.

- **Apps**: Act as logical groupings of resources for a single purpose and result in one or more stacks.

- **Stacks**: Units of deployment, similar to CloudFormation stacks.

- **Environments**: Targets of deployments; can be different regions and/or accounts.

- **Assets**: Local files or Docker images that are bundled with the app. Can be a handler code for Lambda function or a Docker image for an ECS task.

When the template developer starts working with CDK, they need to define each resource as a variable—for example, the definition of the S3 bucket would look like the following.

Don't worry if you don't understand the following code yet! We are going to cover it a bit later:

```python
from aws_cdk import core
import aws_cdk.aws_s3 as s3


class BucketStack(core.Stack):

    def __init__(self, scope: core.Construct, id: str,
**kwargs) -> None:
        super().__init__(scope, id, **kwargs)

        bucket = s3.Bucket(self, "myBucket")

app = core.App()
BucketStack(app, "bucket", env=core.Environment(account="X"))

app.synth()
```

In this code, the stack is actually a Python *class* (`BucketStack`), with necessary construct attributes. We declare a `bucket` variable, which is an object of an `s3.Bucket` type, where `s3` is an imported library, `aws_cdk.aws_s3`. The stack is assigned in a membership of the application, `App`. We also specify the account to which we are going to deploy, but we'll cover this in the next sections.

We will acquire more in-depth knowledge of CDK once we build our own template, but first, let's see how CDK can make our template development life easier.

Facilitating template development with AWS CDK

Why would we choose CDK if we already have extensive experience with CloudFormation? While CloudFormation has a lot of powerful features and deep integration with AWS, its declarative nature may be a burden for those who have just started practicing infrastructure-as-code and AWS.

CloudFormation is simple when you need to create a sample set or resources and want to set most of the properties to the default values. But let's take a look at the full declaration of an S3 bucket:

```
Type: AWS::S3::Bucket
Properties:
  AccelerateConfiguration: ...
  AccessControl: ...
  AnalyticsConfigurations: [ ... ]
  BucketEncryption: ...
  BucketName: ...
  CorsConfiguration: ...
  InventoryConfigurations: [ ... ]
  LifecycleConfiguration: ...
  LoggingConfiguration: ...
  MetricsConfigurations: [ ... ]
  NotificationConfiguration: [ ... ]
  # And counting!..
```

Most of the properties aren't even String or Boolean; those are separate key–value sections that need to be filled. This is not the hardest task to do, but it requires time to find the proper declaration section and not to mess up with YAML or JSON formatting. Adding property blocks or even addition resources may be simpler.

Let's say that we want to have a subnet in a VPC associated with a route table, which has a route to the internet.

Using CloudFormation would include these resources:

```
Vpc:
  Type: AWS::EC2::VPC
  Properties: ...
Igw:
  Type: AWS::EC2::InternetGateway
IgwAttach:
  Type: AWS::EC2::VPCGatewayAttachment
  Properties: ...
Subnet:
  Type: AWS::EC2::Subnet
  Properties: ...
RouteTable:
  Type: AWS::EC2::RouteTable
  Properties: ...
PublicRoute:
  Type: AWS::EC2::Route
  Properties: ...
PublicRouteTableAssoc:
  Type: AWS::EC2::SubnetRouteTableAssociation
  Properties: ...
```

Again, this is the minimum number of resource declarations that we have to do.

Doing this in CDK will be simpler because of its programmatic nature:

```
CIDR = "10.0.0.0/16"
vpc = ec2.Vpc(self,
              "Vpc",
              cidr=CIDR,
              subnet_configuration=[
                  ec2.SubnetConfiguration(name="Public",
subnet_type=ec2.SubnetType.PUBLIC, cidr_mask=24),
                  ec2.SubnetConfiguration(name="Private",
subnet_type=ec2.SubnetType.PRIVATE, cidr_mask=24)
              ])
```

Because CDK has a lot of abstraction inside it, we don't need to explicitly define resources one by one—CDK will do this for us.

Another beneficial feature is that we can use all the abilities of the programming language, such as iterations and conditions.

For example, let's say we want to deploy our stack in multiple regions. We can instruct CDK to create a stack by initializing the Stack class:

```
MyStack(app, "StackName", env= core.Environment(account="X",
                                         region="foo"))
```

Then, we can declare the AWS `regions` and run stack creation, as shown in the following code:

```
regions = ["us-east-1", "eu-west-1", "us-west-1"]
for i in range(len(regions)):
    MyStack(app, f"stack-{i}", env=core.
Environment(account="X", region=regions[i]))
```

This will create multiple stacks, with the stack names `stack-0`, `stack-1`, and `stack-2` all set to be deployed in a single account, but in multiple regions.

Here comes another benefit of CDK: we don't need to use `awscli` to deploy stacks generated by CDK. CDK comes with a set of features and aims to be an all-in-one infrastructure-as-code instrument. We can define our major infrastructure as an application and declare the stacks that will form parts of this application. Once developed and tested, we can deploy all the stacks with a simple command:

```
$ cdk deploy
```

This will deploy the stacks to a target region and account.

Overall, these are the reasons why we could choose to use CDK:

- High-level abstractions create necessary resources for us
- No need to run additional tools such as `awscli`
- We can develop infrastructure in Python or any other programming language that allows us to test software

Let's develop our very first template with CDK.

Writing your first template using AWS CDK and Python

We will begin by installing the prerequisites for CDK. Even though we are going to write our code in Python, we still need to install `nodejs`. Once this is done, we can install CDK:

```
$ npm install -g aws-cdk
```

After this, we need to check whether everything is correct by printing out the version of CDK:

```
$ cdk --version
```

Installing CDK doesn't mean we have all the construct libraries.

First, we need to initialize the environment:

```
$ mkdir app && cd app
$ cdk init app --profile personal --language=python
$ source .env/bin/activate
$ pip install -r requirements.txt
```

Then, we install the core components of CDK:

```
$ pip install --upgrade aws-cdk.core
```

The `cdk init` phrase will create all the files, so we can start developing our infrastructure right away.

Preparing constructs

We will build the same infrastructure that we built in *Chapter 2, Advanced Template Development*. Our infrastructure will consist of the following stacks:

- Core (network, security, and so on)
- Web tier
- Storage tier

We will start by building the core stack, as many resources will be inherited from it.

After running cdk init, we will have created several files and directories.

The main file that will handle generation and deployment is called app.py and looks like this:

app.py

```
from aws_cdk import core
from app.app_stack import AppStack


app = core.App()
AppStack(app, "app")


app.synth()
```

This script initializes the *construct* app and the AppStack class and, in the end, runs the synth() method, which generates the CloudFormation template.

In addition, we have another file that actually has the AppStack class:

app/app_stack.py

```
from aws_cdk import core


class AppStack(core.Stack):


    def __init__(self, scope: core.Construct, id: str,
**kwargs) -> None:
        super().__init__(scope, id, **kwargs)


        # The code that defines your stack goes here
```

This is the class in which we must declare our resources.

> **Important note**
>
> The naming of the files and objects created by CDK might look strange. When we run `cdk init`, it will create an `app.py` file (app here stands for the *App*, the main construct in CDK) and a directory X, where X is the name of the current working directory where you run `cdk init`. In this new directory, `cdk init` will create an `X_stack.py` file and an `XStack()` class. For ease of development and transparency, you should spend time on renaming the files and object accordingly.

CDK created a stack class, but the naming is not what we need here (moreover, we will need multiple classes). So we will rename `app_stack.py` to `core_stack.py` and `AppStack` to `CoreStack`:

app/core_stack.py

```
from aws_cdk import core


class CoreStack(core.Stack):
    # ...
```

We will also make a few changes to `app.py` so that importing works correctly:

app.py

```
from aws_cdk import core
from app.core_stack import CoreStack


app = core.App()
CoreStack(app, "core")


app.synth()
```

We've also made a change in the class initialization call, where we've changed `"app"` to `"core"`:

```
CoreStack(app, "core")
```

The string in quotes stands for Id, a unique identifier for a stack inside CDK. During deployment, this ID will be a stack name, but we made this change now to keep things clearer for us.

We have completed all our preparations. Now, let's begin with the core template.

Rendering core resources

As we will remember, we need the following resources in a core stack:

- 1 VPC
- 3 public subnets
- 3 private subnets
- 1 internet gateway
- 1 NAT gateway
- 1 public route table
- 1 private route table
- 2 IAM roles (for administrators and developers)

CDK doesn't install all construct libraries, so we need to install two of them: aws_ec2 and aws_iam:

```
$ pip install aws_cdk.aws_iam aws_cdk.aws_ec2
```

Now we can import them:

app/core_stack.py

```
from aws_cdk import core
from aws_cdk.core import Fn
import aws_cdk.aws_ec2 as ec2
import aws_cdk.aws_iam as iam
```

By going through the following steps, we will declare the core stack using CDK:

1. Let's start with IAM roles. We create them by declaring variables in a stack class:

app/core_stack.py

```python
# imports...


class CoreStack(core.Stack):


    def __init__(self, scope: core.Construct, id: str,
**kwargs) -> None:
        super().__init__(scope, id, **kwargs)


        admin_role = iam.Role(self,
                              "admin",
                              assumed_by=iam.
AccountPrincipal(Fn.ref("AWS::AccountId")))
        dev_role = iam.Role(self,
                            "developer",
                            assumed_by=iam.
AccountPrincipal(Fn.ref("AWS::AccountId")))
```

Again, we have less code to write, because the `iam.Role` object has an `assumed_by` attribute. This will automatically transform into `AssumeRolePolicyDocument`.

2. To check that everything is generated as expected, we can run `cdk synth`:

```
$ cdk synth
Resources:
  admin81D8EBF0:
    Type: AWS::IAM::Role
    Properties:
      AssumeRolePolicyDocument:
        Statement:
          - Action: sts:AssumeRole
            Effect: Allow
            Principal:
              AWS:
```

```
                  Fn::Join:
                  - ""
                  - - "arn:"
                    - Ref: AWS::Partition
                    - ":iam::"
                    - Ref: AWS::AccountId
                    - :root
          Version: "2012-10-17"
  # the rest of the output...
```

3. The template looks valid, so we can continue by adding policies to our roles:

app/core_stack.py

```python
class CoreStack(core.Stack):

    def __init__(self, scope: core.Construct, id: str,
**kwargs) -> None:
        # ...
        admin_role.add_managed_policy(iam.ManagedPolicy.
from_aws_managed_policy_name("AdministratorAccess"))
        dev_role.add_managed_policy(iam.ManagedPolicy.
from_aws_managed_policy_name("ReadOnlyAccess"))
```

We only need to add managed policies, so we will use an add_managed_policy() method.

4. We can now start building up our network. We will need one public and several private subnets:

```python
class CoreStack(core.Stack):
    # ...
        # VPC section
        self.vpc = ec2.Vpc(self,
                           "vpc",
                           cidr="10.0.0.0/16",
                           enable_dns_hostnames=True,
                           enable_dns_support=True,
                           max_azs=3,
                           nat_gateways=1,
```

```
                                    subnet_configuration=[
                              ec2.
SubnetConfiguration(name="Public", subnet_type=ec2.
SubnetType.PUBLIC, cidr_mask=24),
                              ec2.
SubnetConfiguration(name="Private", subnet_type=ec2.
SubnetType.PRIVATE, cidr_mask=24)
                                    ])
```

There are a few things that we can tweak here. We set `max_azs` to 3 so that we can make sure that our stack can support almost every region (most of the regions have three availability zones). If this number is higher than the number of AZs in a region, then the creation of the stack will fail. We also set `nat_gateways` to 1 so that there will only be a single NAT gateway in a VPC, just to avoid extra costs when we practice using CDK in our personal account (best practice is for there to be one NAT gateway per availability zone).

Each subnet group (public, web, middleware, and storage) is a separate `SubnetConfiguration` object. By using the subnet type of `PUBLIC` or `PRIVATE`, we instruct CDK to configure a proper routing table for subnets (either via internet gateway or NAT gateway).

The main benefit here is that we have defined a single Python `vpc` object, but CDK will generate a lot of resources on our behalf: internet gateway, NAT gateway, subnets, route tables with routes and associations, network ACLs with associations—almost every piece of the core infrastructure that we had to declare manually previously!

We can continue with the rest of the tiers.

Rendering the web tier

The web tier is a stack that is built on top of the core stack. We are going to generate a template that references another stack that we have in mind.

In the web tier, we expect to have the following:

- Application load balancer
- Launch configuration
- Autoscaling group
- A bunch of security groups

In the following code, we are going to generate a declaration of a web tier that uses a part of the resources from the core stack:

1. We start by creating a new file in the same directory where the core stack resides:

app/web_stack.py

```
from aws_cdk import core


class WebStack(core.Stack):


    def __init__(self, scope: core.Construct, id: str,
vpc: ec2.Vpc, **kwargs) -> None:
        super().__init__(scope, id, **kwargs)
```

We added one extra attribute to our class, vpc. This is because we want to inherit properties from the *Core* stack (the same way we would with Exports and Fn::ImportValue).

2. Now we can add resources:

app/web_stack.py

```
class WebStack(core.Stack):


    def __init__(self, scope: core.Construct, id: str,
vpc: ec2.Vpc, **kwargs) -> None:
        super().__init__(scope, id, **kwargs)
        self.vpc = vpc
        asg = autoscaling.AutoScalingGroup(self,
                                            "WebAsg",
                                            instance_
type=ec2.InstanceType.of(ec2.InstanceClass.BURSTABLE2,
ec2.InstanceSize.MICRO),
                                            machine_
image=ec2.AmazonLinuxImage(),
                                            vpc=vpc,
                                            vpc_
subnets=ec2.SubnetSelection(subnet_group_name="Private"),
                                            min_
capacity=1,
```

```
                                      max_capacity=1
                                  )
```

As we can see, some of the properties are not the ones that belong to EC2 autoscaling groups—for example, `instance_type` and `machine_image`. These properties will be used to generate the launch configuration resource.

Moreover, let's take a look at how we provide VPC and subnets for an autoscaling group. What we did is pass the resource construct attribute (`vpc`) from one class (`CoreStack`) to another (`WebStack`).

3. We can see what happens when we add the `WebStack` class to `app.py`:

app.py

```
from aws_cdk import core
from app.core_stack import CoreStack
from app.web_stack import WebStack


app = core.App()
core = CoreStack(app, "core")
web = WebStack(app, "web", vpc=core.vpc)
app.synth()
```

4. Let's run `cdk synth` and check how CDK will assign the resource properties:

```
$ cdk synth web
Including dependency stacks: core
Successfully synthesized to /Users/ktovmasyan/app/cdk.out
Supply a stack id (core, web) to display its template.
```

5. If we evaluate the generated template, we will see the following:

```
{
  "Resources": {
    # some resources...
    "WebAsgASGEE4061A2": {
      "Type": "AWS::AutoScaling::AutoScalingGroup",
      "Properties": {
        # some properties...
```

```
        "VPCZoneIdentifier": [
            {
                "Fn::ImportValue":
"core:ExportsOutputRefvpcPrivateSubnet1Subnet934893E8236
E2271"
            },
            {
                "Fn::ImportValue":
"core:ExportsOutputRefvpcPrivateSubnet2Subnet7031C2BA60
DCB1EE"
            }
        ]
    },
    # the rest of the resources
}
```

What CDK did is *understand* what we are going to do and create exports in the core stack and use them with `Fn::ImportValue`.

> **Important note**
> The best practice with CDK is to expose class fields between stack classes; however, it only works within the same app. If you still need to export values to share between different CDK apps, then you need to use the `CfnOutput` method from `aws_cdk.core`.

6. Let's continue adding resources to our web stack. All we need to do is to add an application load balancer:

app/web_stack.py

```
class WebStack(core.Stack):

    def __init__(self, scope: core.Construct, id: str,
vpc: ec2.Vpc, **kwargs) -> None:
        # ...
        alb = elbv2.ApplicationLoadBalancer(self,
                                            "WebLb",
                                            vpc=vpc,
                                            internet_
```

```
facing=True,
                                          vpc_
subnets=ec2.SubnetSelection(subnet_group_name="Public"))
        listener = alb.add_listener("WebListener",
                                  port=80)
        listener.add_targets("Target",
                           port=80,
                           targets=[asg])
```

We don't need to create a target group separately. When we use the
`add_targets()` method, CDK will automatically declare a target group
and refer to it from both the listener and autoscaling group.

7. Before we continue with a storage tier, let's deploy the web stacks to check that our
code is operational:

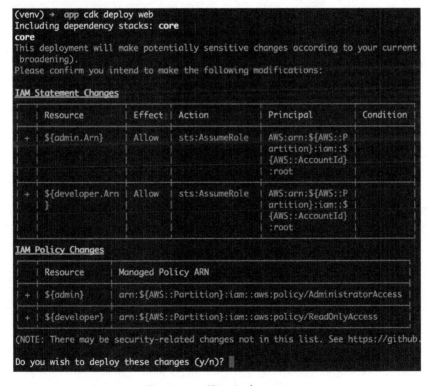

Figure 9.1 – Terminal output

Since the core is a dependency stack, it will be deployed first. What we are interested in is to construct a setup where CDK informs us of security-related changes, such as the IAM and security groups rule, as shown in the following code:

```
IAM Statement Changes

  Resource                            Effect   Action         Principal                     Condition

+ ${WebAsg/InstanceRole.Arn}         Allow    sts:AssumeRole  Service:ec2.${AWS::URLSuffix}

Security Group Changes

  Group                                            Dir   Protocol     Peer

+ ${WebAsg/InstanceSecurityGroup.GroupId}         In    TCP 80       ${WebLb/SecurityGroup.GroupId}
+ ${WebAsg/InstanceSecurityGroup.GroupId}         Out   Everything   Everyone (IPv4)

+ ${WebLb/SecurityGroup.GroupId}                  In    TCP 80       Everyone (IPv4)
+ ${WebLb/SecurityGroup.GroupId}                  Out   TCP 80       ${WebAsg/InstanceSecurityGroup.GroupId}

(NOTE: There may be security-related changes not in this list. See https://github.com/aws/aws-cdk/issues/1299)

Do you wish to deploy these changes (y/n)?
```

Figure 9.2 – Terminal output

Another interesting thing to point out is that when we associate an autoscaling group with an application load balancer, CDK will automatically add a security group rule to allow incoming traffic to a traffic port *only* from a load balancer's security group.

Let's also install some software on our launch configurations using user data.

8. We will declare `userdata` as a multiline string variable:

app/web_stack.py

```
userdata = '''#!/bin/sh
          yum install httpd -y
          systemctl enable httpd
          systemctl start httpd
          echo "<html><head><title> Example Web
Server</title></head>" >  /var/www/html/index.html
          echo "<body>" >>  /var/www/html/index.html
          echo "<div><center><h2>Welcome AWS
$(hostname -f) </h2>" >>  /var/www/html/index.html
          echo "<hr/>" >>  /var/www/html/index.html
          curl http://169.254.169.254/latest/meta-
data/instance-id >> /var/www/html/index.html
          echo "</center></div></body></html>" >>  /
var/www/html/index.html'''
```

9.   Then, we process it via CDK and pass it as an attribute to the autoscaling group:

app/web_stack.py

```
class WebStack(core.Stack):

    def __init__(self, scope: core.Construct, id: str,
vpc: ec2.Vpc, **kwargs) -> None:
        super().__init__(scope, id, **kwargs)
        self.vpc = vpc
        userdata = "..."
        websrv = ec2.UserData.for_linux()
        websrv.add_commands(userdata)
        asg = autoscaling.AutoScalingGroup(self,
                                            #some
attributes...
                                            user_
data=websrv)
```

There is one small thing that we need to add to the web tier. Since we don't want to expose our RDS instance to the public, we want it to be accessible only from the web servers.

10.   To do this, we will create a security group and add it to the autoscaling group construct:

app/web_stack.py

```
class WebStack(core.Stack):

    def __init__(self, scope: core.Construct, id: str,
vpc: ec2.Vpc, **kwargs) -> None:
        super().__init__(scope, id, **kwargs)
        # resources ...
        self.webserver_sg = ec2.SecurityGroup(self,
"WebServerSg", vpc=vpc)
        asg.add_security_group(self.webserver_sg)
```

After this, our autoscaling group will have two security groups: one that we assigned at the creation of the autoscaling group (between the load balancer and the autoscaling group) and one that we declared right now.

We have finished the generation of our web tier, containing the application load balancer and the autoscaling group, so we can continue with the storage tier.

Rendering the storage tier

Our storage tier will be an RDS instance, created in a VPC from a core stack:

1. We will create a new stack class in a separate file:

app/rds_stack.py

```python
from aws_cdk import core
import aws_cdk.aws_ec2 as ec2
import aws_cdk.aws_rds as rds


class RdsStack(core.Stack):
    def __init__(self, scope: core.Construct, id: str,
vpc: ec2.Vpc, webserver_sg: ec2.SecurityGroup, **kwargs)
-> None:
        super().__init__(scope, id, **kwargs)
        self.vpc = vpc
        self.webserver_sg = webserver_sg
```

We added two extra fields to a class declaration: vpc (we will use a VPC construct from the core stack) and webserver_sg (the security group construct we declared at the end of the previous section).

2. There is not much that we need to do with RDS—just create an RDS instance and add a rule to its security group:

app/rds_stack.py

```python
class RdsStack(core.Stack):
    def __init__(self, scope: core.Construct, id: str,
vpc: ec2.Vpc, webserver_sg: ec2.SecurityGroup, **kwargs)
-> None:
        # Avoid hardcoding password in production!
        # Instead - try using Secrets Manager with
        # random string generation.
        pw = core.SecretValue.plain_text("password")
        rds_instance = rds.DatabaseInstance(
            self, "Rds",
            master_username="user",
            master_user_password=pw,
```

```
                database_name="db",
                engine=rds.DatabaseInstanceEngine.MYSQL,
                vpc=vpc,
                instance_class=ec2.InstanceType.of(
                        ec2.InstanceClass.BURSTABLE2,
                        ec2.InstanceSize.MICRO),
                removal_policy=core.RemovalPolicy.DESTROY,
                deletion_protection=False)
        rds_instance.connections.allow_from(
                webserver_sg,
                ec2.Port.tcp(3306))
```

That will create a set of resources—a DB subnet group, an RDS instance with a security group to which the new rule will be added. Because we refer to a field from another class (the web tier), CDK will create an export with a security group ID.

3. Lastly, we are going to add a new class to app.py:

app.py

```
from aws_cdk import core
from app.core_stack import CoreStack
from app.web_stack import WebStack
from app.rds_stack import RdsStack

app = core.App()
core = CoreStack(app, "core")
web = WebStack(app, "web", vpc=core.vpc)
rds = RdsStack(app, "rds", vpc=core.vpc, webserver_
sg=web.webserver_sg)
app.synth()
```

We have added all three stacks to our application, so now we can begin deployment.

Deploying CDK application

The deployment of CDK applications is done by means of the cdk deploy command. This command will run synth to generate the CloudFormation template and then create and execute a change set.

If we have any security-related resources (such as security groups and IAM entities), then CDK will request our confirmation. If we want to avoid this (for example, when deployment is done as part of the CI/CD pipeline), we can use the `--require approval never` argument.

We can deploy stacks one by one, as shown in the following code:

```
$ cdk deploy core
$ cdk deploy web
$ cdk deploy rds
```

However, our RDS stack has a dependency on the core and web. So if we just run deployment on this, CDK will attempt to deploy all dependencies first:

```
$ cdk deploy rds
Including dependency stacks: core, web
# the rest of the output
```

The deployment of the CDK application has an interactive response. This means that we can continuously observe the current state of the CloudFormation deployment:

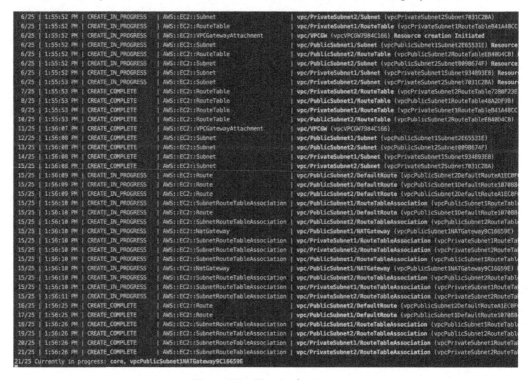

Figure 9.3 – Terminal output

By the end of the deployment, we will see the confirmation message that the stacks have been deployed. CDK will also print the stack ARN and outputs to the terminal:

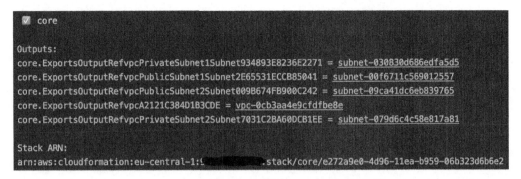

Figure 9.4 – Terminal output

If we need to delete all stacks, then we simply need to run cdk destroy. Since we are going to delete multiple stacks, we need to destroy a main dependency, which is the core stack:

```
$ cdk destroy core
Including depending stacks: web, rds
Are you sure you want to delete: rds, web, core (y/n)?
```

Once we select y, CDK will destroy all the stacks in reverse order.

We've covered the deployment and deletion of CDK applications. Now, let's learn about another important topic—testing CDK applications

Testing CDK applications

Until now, the only way of testing CloudFormation has been either by creating a stack and running some tests against resources or by conducting an inspection with cfn-lint using custom rules.

In CDK, testing is done in the same way as common software testing, but against the stack classes and its attributes.

> **Important note**
> At the time of writing, testing CDK code with native CDK testing libraries is only available for code written in TypeScript.

Since we can't use CDK's assertion library with Python, we will write our own tests using `unittests`:

1. We will create a test skeleton first:

```
tests/test_app.py
import unittest


class StackCase(unittest.TestCase):
    def test_True(self):
        self.assertTrue(True)


if __name__ == '__main__':
    unittest.main()
```

2. Let's make sure our test skeleton works correctly:

```
$ python tests/test_app.py
.
-----------------------------------------------------------
-----Ran 1 test in 0.000s

OK
```

We can start adding tests now. We will begin with the critical part of our application - the network.

3. Let's test whether our VPC has public subnets:

tests/test_app.py

```
import unittest
from app.core_stack import CoreStack
import aws_cdk.aws_ec2 as ec2
import aws_cdk.core as core
```

```
class StackCase(unittest.TestCase):


    def test_if_vpc_has_public_subnets(self):
        app = core.App()
        core_construct = CoreStack(app, "core")
        selected_subnets = core_construct.vpc.select_
subnets(
            subnet_type=ec2.SubnetType.PUBLIC)
        self.assertTrue(selected_subnets.has_public)
```

What we are going to test is whether the vpc construct will return True when we check the attributes of selected subnets with the PUBLIC subnet type. To do so, we initialize the app object and the core construct. After they are initialized, we read the attributes of the vpc object and see whether it has public subnets.

4. Let's run this test:

```
$ python tests/test_app.py -v
test_if_vpc_has_public_subnets (__main__.StackCase) ...
ok


------------------------------------------------------------
----Ran 1 test in 0.057s


OK
```

5. Let's do the same for private subnets:

tests/test_app.py

```
class StackCase(unittest.TestCase):
# previous tests...
    def test_if_vpc_has_private_subnets(self):
        app = core.App()
        core_construct = CoreStack(app, "core")
        selected_subnets = core_construct.vpc.select_
subnets(
            subnet_type=ec2.SubnetType.PRIVATE)
        self.assertFalse(selected_subnets.has_public)
```

6. And now let's run it again:

```
$ python tests/test_app.py -v
test_if_vpc_has_private_subnets (__main__.StackCase) ...
ok
test_if_vpc_has_public_subnets (__main__.StackCase) ...
ok


----------------------------------------------------------
-----Ran 2 tests in 0.088s

OK
```

7. We could also check that our developer role doesn't have AdministratorAccess.
    This will be a bit difficult, because we can't access managed policies from the role
    class directly, so we will have to generate a template and then parse it:

tests/test_app.py

```python
class StackCase(unittest.TestCase):


    def test_if_dev_role_is_not_admin(self):
        app = core.App()
        CoreStack(app, "core")
        stack = app.synth()
        core_stack = stack.get_stack_by_name("core").
template
        resources = core_stack['Resources']
        for resource in resources.keys():
            if str(resource).startswith("developer"):
                developer_role = resource
        self.assertNotEqual(
            "[{'Fn::Join': ['', ['arn:',
{'Ref': 'AWS::Partition'}, ':iam::aws:policy/
AdministratorAccess']]}]",
            str(resources[developer_role]['Properties']
['ManagedPolicyArns']))
```

We have to partially match the `developer` resource because CDK adds some encoded string after it. Once we locate the resource in the template, we make sure that its `ManagedPolicyArns` property doesn't equal the same line in the generated template.

8. Let's run all the tests again:

```
$ python tests/test_app.py -v
test_if_dev_role_is_not_admin (__main__.StackCase) ... ok
test_if_vpc_has_private_subnets (__main__.StackCase) ...
ok
test_if_vpc_has_public_subnets (__main__.StackCase) ...
ok


----------------------------------------------------------------
----Ran 3 tests in 0.183s

OK
```

We are now able to run tests against our CDK code before actually deploying it. This will make our infrastructure provisioning even more secure and reliable!

In this section, we have covered all the steps for working with CDK, from initialization of the CDK project to writing the multitier infrastructure declaration, deploying it, and even writing the test suite for it!

Summary

CDK introduces a new way of managing AWS and allows us to create templates and run stack operations in a completely different way.

In this chapter, we've learned about CDK and its capabilities. We've created our applications with multiple stacks and created a test suite to make sure that our core infrastructure template is operational before deployment.

CDK is useful for those cases where the AWS engineer role is handled by developers who have a good knowledge of software engineering and who want to use this knowledge together with CloudFormation automation.

In the next chapter, we will cover another extension of CloudFormation called **SAM—Serverless Application Model**. SAM is similar to CloudFormation, but offers a different approach for developing serverless applications.

See you in the next chapter!

Questions

1. What are constructs in CDK?

2. How is it possible to have multiple stacks within a single application?

3. How can we declare private and public subnets for VPC in CDK?

4. Which programming languages are currently supported by CDK?

5. Is it mandatory to add an AWS account ID in CDK?

Further reading

- AWS CDK samples: `https://github.com/aws-samples/aws-cdk-examples`

- Testing infrastructure with AWS CDK: `https://aws.amazon.com/blogs/developer/testing-infrastructure-with-the-aws-cloud-development-kit-cdk/`

10
Deploying Serverless Applications Using AWS SAM

CloudFormation is a powerful instrument. However, as new technologies and ways of working emerge, new requirements appear for **Infrastructure-as-Code (IaC)** tools. After the release of Lambda and its integration with other AWS services, including S3, SNS, SQS, and DynamoDB, it appeared that most of CloudFormation's capabilities were not required for serverless development.

So, a **Serverless Application Model (SAM)** was developed. SAM introduces a different and more simplified way of developing, building, testing, deploying, and operating serverless applications. In this chapter, we are going to learn about SAM and how to use it to facilitate the development of serverless applications.

In this chapter, we will cover the following topics:

- Introducing AWS SAM
- Understanding the differences between SAM and CloudFormation
- Writing your first serverless applications with SAM

Technical requirements

The code used in this chapter can be found in this book's GitHub repository at `https://github.com/PacktPublishing/Mastering-AWS-CloudFormation/tree/master/Chapter10`.

Check out the following video to see the Code in Action:

`https://bit.ly/2yWn7al`

Introducing AWS SAM

Before we learn about SAM, let's quickly look at what serverless is. *Serverless* is a way of developing, running, and operating applications without needing to manage its underlying infrastructure. You might wonder what the key difference is since you don't manage *any* infrastructure in AWS, and you would be right.

You don't have to manage any physical infrastructure in AWS, but if you run an EC2 instance, you need to take care of its underlying OSes, security, patches, and updates.

Then, you will need to consider AWS's managed **Relational Database Service** (**RDS**), where you don't have to worry about the underlying OS, but you still have to tweak its parameters, carry out performance tuning by reorganizing queries and tables, and create database indexes.

Serverless doesn't guarantee that no operational work will be required, but there are several differences between instance-based services (such as EC2, RDS, EMR, and MSK) and serverless services (such as S3, SNS, SQS, Lambda, and DynamoDB).

With serverless services, the following points stand:

- You pay only for the storage ($ per GB) and the actual compute operation (number of requests).
- You don't operate with instances, but with compute and storage units.
- You work with specific entities (such as functions instead of whole runtimes or tables instead of whole databases).

These core concepts are what make serverless computing cost-efficient for many business cases.

SAM was introduced to fully support the development, packaging, and deployment of serverless applications using IaC as its approach.

SAM consists of two parts:

- The actual framework (the CLI that performs all the operations)

- A template, which has similar specifications to CloudFormation

Similar to CDK, SAM can perform all of its operations out of the box, such as building, testing locally, and provisioning serverless stacks to AWS.

SAM templates are easier to write due to their restricted abilities. For example, a DynamoDB table definition looks like the following:

```
Transform: AWS::Serverless-2016-10-31
Resources:
  DynamoDb:
    Type: AWS::Serverless::SimpleTable
    Properties:
      TableName: myTable
      PrimaryKey:
        Name: id
        Type: string
```

Does the Transform: AWS::Serverless-2016-10-31 line look familiar?

Remember from *Chapter 8, Dynamically Rendering the Template Using Template Macros*, that AWS has two internal macros: AWS::Serverless and AWS::Include. The SAM template, on its own, is nothing but a macro template that will be processed during deployment by CloudFormation. The previous template will look different after transformation, as shown:

```
{
  "Resources": {
    "DynamoDb": {
      "Type": "AWS::DynamoDB::Table",
      "Properties": {
        "KeySchema": [
          {
            "KeyType": "HASH",
            "AttributeName": "id"
          }
        ],
```

```
        "TableName": "myTable",
        "AttributeDefinitions": [
            {
                "AttributeName": "id",
                "AttributeType": "S"
            }
        ],
        "BillingMode": "PAY_PER_REQUEST"
        }
      }
    }
  }
```

SimpleTable in SAM is the same as a DynamoDB table in CloudFormation!

We will cover more on SAM when we start building our own applications, but for now, let's compare SAM and CloudFormation, so we can get the most out of both.

Understanding the differences between SAM and CloudFormation

First of all, a SAM template is designed to be used with serverless applications and services. At the time of writing, the SAM template reference supports the following resource types:

- AWS::Serverless::API: Creates an API gateway and related resources

- AWS::Serverless::Application: Creates a serverless application

- AWS::Serverless::Function: Creates a Lambda function and related resources

- AWS::Serverless::HttpApi: Creates an HTTP API gateway and related resources

- AWS::Serverless::LayerVersion: Creates a Lambda layer

- AWS::Serverless::SimpleTable: Creates a simplified DynamoDB table (only a primary key without a sort key)

It is still possible to combine CloudFormation's resources with SAM's resources. For example, if we want to create an S3 bucket with `SimpleTable`, we can do so by adding the CloudFormation resource, as in the following code:

```
Transform: AWS::Serverless-2016-10-31
Resources:
  DynamoDb:
    Type: AWS::Serverless::SimpleTable
    Properties:
      TableName: myTable
      PrimaryKey:
        Name: id
        Type: string
  Bucket:
    Type: AWS::S3::Bucket
```

All we need to do is to specify the CloudFormation-specific resource types.

Secondly, you *must* have a bucket when you want to deploy a SAM application via a CLI and without interactive dialog. The reason for this is that SAM applications consist of source code and a template. The SAM CLI will take care of building the application, if it requires compilations, and will upload the artifact for your Lambda function to S3.

Thirdly, you can't use the SAM CLI to delete a SAM application. You will have to run `aws cloudformation delete-stack` in order to clean up.

Last but not least, SAM allows you to run tests locally by creating a local API gateway or running test events against your applications.

That said, let's start by building our own serverless applications with SAM.

Writing your first serverless application with SAM

In this section, we will create a few serverless applications to cover most of SAM's capabilities. The first one—Hello, World—will be created using AWS Quick Start templates, so we can quickly get hands-on experience with SAM.

The second—Party Planner—will be developed from scratch. You don't have to worry—the actual code is not in the scope of this book and the actual focus will be on creating a complex application with more than one function.

Before we begin development, let's make sure we have everything we need.

Prerequisites

In order to run the SAM commands, we need to install SAM and its dependencies first. Depending on the OS you have, the steps will be different. The following steps are for installation on macOS.

The guides on how to install SAM on other OSes can be found at `https://docs.aws.amazon.com/serverless-application-model/latest/developerguide/serverless-sam-cli-install.html`.

The following steps show you how to install SAM:

1. Make sure you have Docker and Homebrew installed.

2. Install the SAM CLI by issuing the following commands:

```
$ brew tap aws/tap
$ brew install aws-sam-cli
```

3. Check the installation by running the following command :

```
$ sam --version
```

If you don't see any errors in the output, you are good to go!

We have everything installed, so let's start to build our first application.

Developing a Hello, World application

What is the best entry point, if not a good old Hello, World application? By the end of this section, we will deploy a standard AWS Quick Start application so that we can get some hands-on experience with SAM:

1. We are going to start with the project initialization:

```
$ sam init
```

2. SAM will respond with a dialog. Since it is our very first application, let's follow it. We will choose 1 - AWS Quick Start Templates this time:

```
Which template source would you like to use?
        1 - AWS Quick Start Templates
        2 - Custom Template Location
Choice: 1
```

3. Next, we need to choose the runtime for our application. Let's choose python3.8:

```
Which runtime would you like to use?
        1 - nodejs12.x
        2 - python3.8
        3 - ruby2.5
        4 - go1.x
        5 - java11
        # the rest of the options...
Runtime: 2
```

4. For the application name, simply enter hello-world:

```
Project name [sam-app]: hello-world
```

5. SAM will clone the templates from GitHub and ask us to choose a Quick Start template. We will go for Hello World Example:

```
AWS quick start application templates:
        1 - Hello World Example
        2 - EventBridge Hello World
        3 - EventBridge App from scratch (100+ Event
Schemas)
Template selection: 1
```

6. After all the responses, SAM will generate an app and inform us of the next steps:

```
-----------------------
Generating application:
-----------------------
```

```
Name: hello-world
Runtime: python3.8
Dependency Manager: pip
Application Template: hello-world
Output Directory: .

Next steps can be found in the README file at ./hello-
world/README.md
```

7. Let's examine the new directory:

```
$ tree .

.
├── README.md
├── __init__.py
├── events
│   └── event.json
├── hello_world
│   ├── __init__.py
│   ├── app.py
│   └── requirements.txt
├── template.yaml
└── tests
    ├── __init__.py
    └── unit
        ├── __init__.py
        └── test_handler.py
```

Looks like we have everything set! We could deploy this application right away but first, let's examine what is in the template! There are a few things that look interesting:

template.yaml

```
Globals:
  Function:
    Timeout: 3
```

The `Globals` section is used when we need to define the same properties for multiple resources. Let's say you are building a Lambda application consisting of multiple functions. All of them will use the same runtime and have the same timeout. In order to avoid duplicating the same property many times, we can just store them in `Globals`.

Let's look at our Lambda function:

template.yaml

```
Resources:
  HelloWorldFunction:
    Type: AWS::Serverless::Function
    Properties:
      CodeUri: hello_world/
      Handler: app.lambda_handler
      Runtime: python3.8
      Events:
        HelloWorld:
          Type: Api
          Properties:
            Path: /hello
            Method: get
```

What we can learn from here is that the `function` definition has a `CodeUri` property, which points to the local path where our source code exists.

Secondly, take a look at the `Events` property. This property defines the event source that will trigger the function. Moreover, SAM will *create* this resource when the application is deployed! In this case, it will create an API gateway.

Lastly, take a look at `Outputs`:

template.yaml

```
Outputs:
  HelloWorldApi:
    Description: "API Gateway endpoint URL for Prod stage
for Hello World function"
    Value: !Sub "https://${ServerlessRestApi}.execute-
api.${AWS::Region}.amazonaws.com/Prod/hello/"
```

```
    HelloWorldFunction:
       Description: "Hello World Lambda Function ARN"
       Value: !GetAtt HelloWorldFunction.Arn
    HelloWorldFunctionIamRole:
       Description: "Implicit IAM Role created for Hello
    World function"
       Value: !GetAtt HelloWorldFunctionRole.Arn
```

The API at the top is created as part of the Events property. However, the IAM role wasn't defined anywhere, so how can we get its attribute?

Remember that SAM is a macro. This role (and many other resources) will be created along with the function, which is declared in this template.

8. Next, let's build this application and run local tests:

```
$ sam build --use-container
Starting Build inside a container
Building resource 'HelloWorldFunction'
Fetching lambci/lambda:build-python3.8 Docker container
image....
Mounting /Users/karentovmasyan/hello-world/hello_world as
/tmp/samcli/source:ro,delegated inside runtime container
Build Succeeded
Built Artifacts   : .aws-sam/build
Built Template    : .aws-sam/build/template.yaml
Commands you can use next
=========================
[*] Invoke Function: sam local invoke
[*] Deploy: sam deploy --guided
Running PythonPipBuilder:ResolveDependencies
Running PythonPipBuilder:CopySource
```

The build command, with a --use-container argument, will pull a Docker image and build the source function, thereby installing all the dependencies. The artifact will be stored in a local directory.

9. Let's invoke it:

```
$ sam local invoke
Invoking app.lambda_handler (python3.8)
```

```
Fetching lambci/lambda:python3.8 Docker container
image...
```

```
Mounting /Users/karentovmasyan/hello-world/.aws-sam/
build/HelloWorldFunction as /var/task:ro,delegated inside
runtime container
```

```
START RequestId: c165be27-ff86-1ed2-f5c7-9158dce5d95b
Version: $LATEST
```

```
END RequestId: c165be27-ff86-1ed2-f5c7-9158dce5d95b
```

```
REPORT RequestId: c165be27-ff86-1ed2-f5c7-9158dce5d95b
Init Duration: 199.95 ms          Duration: 3.57 ms
Billed Duration: 100 ms Memory Size: 128 MB        Max
Memory Used: 23 MB
```

```
{"statusCode":200,"body":"{\"message\": \"hello
world\"}"}
```

We don't need to provide many arguments to a local invocation since there is only a single Lambda function and a single event. However, if we had various events and functions, we would have needed to specify them by name, as follows:

```
$ sam local invoke FunctionNameAsInTemplate \
                              --event path/to/the/
event.json
```

What we also get before the actual response is the duration and memory information of the Lambda execution. This comes in handy when we need to estimate the cost of a future serverless application.

There is also another way to test the function execution. Let's do the same with a call to the API gateway.

10. We will start the API:

```
$ sam local start-api
```

In the output, there will be a URL that we can invoke. We have to use a different terminal window because the current one will show the logs of the API gateway:

```
$ curl localhost:3000/hello
```

```
{"message": "hello world"}
```

While in the logs of the API gateway, we will see a similar output as when we ran a local invocation.

We've played around enough—let's now run this application in the cloud!

Running SAM applications

Creating and running SAM applications is a bit different to creating a CloudFormation stack.

Following the previous steps, we will launch our Hello, World application:

1. We are going to package our application:

    ```
    $ aws s3 mb s3://mastering-cfn-sam-bucket
    # your bucket name might differ!
    $ sam package \
        --s3-bucket mastering-cfn-sam-bucket
    ```

    The last command will package the Lambda function and its dependencies, upload them to S3, and then replace `CodeUri` with a new value (pointing to the S3 object):

    ```
    AWSTemplateFormatVersion: '2010-09-09'
    Transform: AWS::Serverless-2016-10-31
    # ...
    Resources:
      HelloWorldFunction:
        Type: AWS::Serverless::Function
        Properties:
          CodeUri: s3://mastering-cfn-sam-bucket/849dd527a4c6
    568a34af04808b924158
          Handler: app.lambda_handler
          Runtime: python3.8
    # the rest of the template...
    ```

2. In order to store this template locally and use it for deployment, we need to add one extra argument:

    ```
    sam package \
        --s3-bucket mastering-cfn-sam-bucket \
        --output-template-file template-out.yaml
    ```

    This will store the template in a working directory and provide us with the command that we need to use to create a stack with the application:

    ```
    Successfully packaged artifacts and wrote output template
    to file template-out.yaml.
    ```

```
Execute the following command to deploy the packaged
template
sam deploy --template-file /Users/karentovmasyan/
MasteringCloudformation/Chapter10/hello-world/template-
out.yaml --stack-name <YOUR STACK NAME>
```

Let's deploy it using the preceding command:

```
$ sam deploy \
      --template-file template-out.yaml \
      --stack-name hello-world


      Deploying with following values
      =================================
      Stack name                   : hello-world
      Region                       : None
      Confirm changeset            : False
      Deployment s3 bucket         : None
      Capabilities                 : null
      Parameter overrides          : {}


Initiating deployment
=====================
Error: Failed to create changeset for the stack: hello-
world, Parameter validation failed:
Invalid type for parameter Capabilities, value: None,
type: <class 'NoneType'>, valid types: <class 'list'>,
<class 'tuple'>
```

The reason it failed is because SAM will create an IAM role, but we haven't provided any capabilities.

3. Let's fix this by adding the necessary capabilities with a command-line argument:

```
$ sam deploy \
      --template-file template-out.yaml \
      --stack-name hello-world \
      --capabilities CAPABILITY_IAM
```

In the output, we will see something similar to the CDK deployments—the resources that SAM is going to create, the event log, and the outputs:

```
CloudFormation stack changeset
-------------------------------------------------------------------------------
Operation                LogicalResourceId              ResourceType
-------------------------------------------------------------------------------
+ Add                    HelloWorldFunctionHelloWorldPe AWS::Lambda::Permission
                         rmissionProd
+ Add                    HelloWorldFunctionRole         AWS::IAM::Role
+ Add                    HelloWorldFunction             AWS::Lambda::Function
+ Add                    ServerlessRestApiDeployment47f AWS::ApiGateway::Deployment
                         c2d5f9d
+ Add                    ServerlessRestApiProdStage     AWS::ApiGateway::Stage
+ Add                    ServerlessRestApi              AWS::ApiGateway::RestApi
```

Figure 10.1 – The terminal output (resources)

We can follow the deployment process by examining the events right from the terminal output:

```
CloudFormation events from changeset
-------------------------------------------------------------------------------
ResourceStatus       ResourceType         LogicalResourceId      ResourceStatusReason
-------------------------------------------------------------------------------
CREATE_IN_PROGRESS   AWS::IAM::Role       HelloWorldFunctionRole Resource creation
                                                                 Initiated
CREATE_IN_PROGRESS   AWS::IAM::Role       HelloWorldFunctionRole -
CREATE_COMPLETE      AWS::IAM::Role       HelloWorldFunctionRole -
CREATE_IN_PROGRESS   AWS::Lambda::Function HelloWorldFunction    -
CREATE_IN_PROGRESS   AWS::Lambda::Function HelloWorldFunction    Resource creation
                                                                 Initiated
CREATE_COMPLETE      AWS::Lambda::Function HelloWorldFunction    -
CREATE_IN_PROGRESS   AWS::ApiGateway::RestA ServerlessRestApi    -
                     pi
CREATE_COMPLETE      AWS::ApiGateway::RestA ServerlessRestApi    -
                     pi
CREATE_IN_PROGRESS   AWS::ApiGateway::RestA ServerlessRestApi    Resource creation
                     pi                                          Initiated
CREATE_IN_PROGRESS   AWS::Lambda::Permissio HelloWorldFunctionHell -
```

Figure 10.2 – The terminal output (events)

4. Lastly, let's invoke our API to make sure that the application deployment was successful:

```
$ curl https://39llxp6wl2.execute-api.eu-central-1.
amazonaws.com/Prod/hello/ # your output will be different
{"message": "hello world"}
```

That's it! We have an application running on an AWS environment that was developed and deployed using AWS SAM.

But that's not the only thing that SAM can do! In addition to building and deploying operations, it can be used to examine application logs.

Examining logs with SAM

SAM allows you to fetch CloudWatch logs right from the CLI. It makes debugging or tracking an application in production a bit easier.

To read the logs, we only need to provide the following arguments:

```
$ sam logs \
    -n FUNCTION_LOGICAL_NAME \
    --stack-name STACK_NAME \
    --tail
```

So, for our case, we will run the command as follows:

```
$ sam logs \
    -n HelloWorldFunction \
    --stack-name hello-world \
    --tail
```

Once we run it, we will get the exact entries from CloudWatch Logs. Since there are no print statements in our function code, the logs won't show us that much:

```
2020-02-18T14:12:54.944000 START RequestId: 4dd811f0-79a6-4806-a8cc-26d2e0da9543 Version: $LATEST
2020-02-18T14:12:54.951000 END RequestId: 4dd811f0-79a6-4806-a8cc-26d2e0da9543
2020-02-18T14:12:54.951000 REPORT RequestId: 4dd811f0-79a6-4806-a8cc-26d2e0da9543  Duration: 1.75 ms

2020-02-18T14:13:01.379000 START RequestId: cc85630f-a1f0-4d52-9d77-65248adfb102 Version: $LATEST
2020-02-18T14:13:01.382000 END RequestId: cc85630f-a1f0-4d52-9d77-65248adfb102
2020-02-18T14:13:01.382000 REPORT RequestId: cc85630f-a1f0-4d52-9d77-65248adfb102  Duration: 1.43 ms
```

Figure 10.3 – The terminal output (the SAM logs)

To clean up the `hello-world` stack, we need to use `awscli`:

```
$ aws cloudformation delete-stack \
                --stack-name hello-world
```

We're now done with playing around with the Hello, World application. Let's build something more complex—our second application.

Creating complex applications with SAM

We are going to create a small party planner—an application that will process and store information about parties and guests.

Let's take a look at the design of this app:

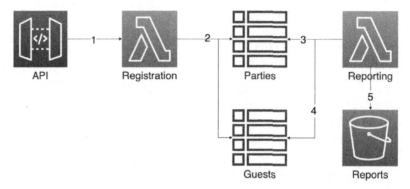

Figure 10.4 – A serverless party planner

There are several steps in this application:

1. The **API** gateway will send a payload with the party and guest information.

2. The **Registration** function will create a new entry in a **Parties** table, if this party doesn't exist, and will store guest information (such as names and dietary restrictions).

3. The **Reporting** function will check whether there is a party in the future (the party date is not in the past).

4. The **Reporting** function (a scheduled task) will get the guest information and generate a planning report.

5. The **Reporting** function will store this report in an S3 bucket.

We know what our application looks like and what it is expected to do. Let's build it now using SAM!

We will begin by creating the project structure:

```
$ mkdir registration reporting
$ touch template.yaml
```

Next, we need to define the resources for our template. We will need the following resources:

- Two Lambda functions (**Registration** and **Reporting**)
- One S3 bucket (**Reports**)
- Two DynamoDB tables (**Parties** and **Guests**)
- One API gateway

Remember that Lambda functions are defined with a different type (AWS::Serverless::Function). We will create the function using this type, so we can create event triggers (the API gateway, in our case) as part of this resource.

The following steps will help us to achieve the goal of this section:

1. Let's declare the Registration function in a template:

template.yaml

```
Resources:
  RegistrationFunction:
    Type: AWS::Serverless::Function
    Properties:
      CodeUri: registration/
      Events:
        register:
          Type: Api
          Properties:
            Path: /register
            Method: post
```

This function is similar to the one we created as part of the Hello, World application. However, there are a few extra things we need to add to it.

The SAM stack will also have RegistrationFunctionRole, which is an IAM role with basic IAM policies for the Lambda function. We also need to have a policy that allows our function to put items in DynamoDB.

2. We will create the tables first:

template.yaml

```yaml
Resources:
  # ...
  PartiesTable:
    Type: AWS::Serverless::SimpleTable
    Properties:
      PrimaryKey:
        Name: PartyName
        Type: String

  GuestsTable:
    Type: AWS::Serverless::SimpleTable
    Properties:
      PrimaryKey:
        Name: GuestName
        Type: String
```

3. Now, we can add an extra policy for our function to access these tables:

template.yaml

```yaml
Resources:
  RegistrationFunction:
    Type: AWS::Serverless::Function
    Properties:
      # ...
      Policies:
        Statement:
          - Effect: Allow
            Action:
              - dynamodb:PutItem
              - dynamodb:GetItem
            Resource:
              - !Sub
```

```
          b:${AWS::Region}:${AWS::AccountId}:table/${PartiesTable}"
                     - !Sub
          db:${AWS::Region}:${AWS::AccountId}:table/${GuestsTable}"
```

Since `AWS::Serverless::SimpleTable` doesn't return the ARN of the DynamoDB table, we have to generate it using `Fn::Sub`.

4. We also need to create a bucket where we will store our reports:

template.yaml

```
Resources:
  # ...
  ReportsBucket:
    Type: AWS::S3::Bucket
```

Don't forget that we will use CloudFormation's type for that since S3 is not part of SAM's specification.

Lastly, we will declare a reporting function with a few differences.

5. The first difference is the policy since we require different IAM privileges for the `Reporting` function to work:

template.yaml

```
Resources:
  # ...
  ReportingFunction:
    # ...
    Policies:
      Statement:
        - Effect: Allow
          Action:
            - dynamodb:GetItem
            - dynamodb:Scan
          Resource:
            - !Sub
          b:${AWS::Region}:${AWS::AccountId}:table/${PartiesTable}"
            - !Sub
          db:${AWS::Region}:${AWS::AccountId}:table/${GuestsTable}"
        - Effect: Allow
```

```
      Action:
         - s3:ListBucket
         - s3:GetBucketAcl
         - s3:PutObject
      Resource:
         - !GetAtt ReportsBucket.Arn
         - !Sub "${ReportsBucket.Arn}/*"
```

Next, we need to change the event since this function is a scheduled job. The only way to run scheduled jobs in Lambda is to use CloudWatch scheduled events.

6. We add a scheduled event by using a different type for Events:

template.yaml

```
Resources:
# ...
  ReportingFunction:
    Type: AWS::Serverless::Function
    Properties:
      # ...
      Events:
        scheduled:
          Type: Schedule
          Properties:
            Schedule: "rate(1 day)"
```

This will create a scheduled event with a generated name and map it to the Reporting function.

The code for the application is not in the scope of this book, but the functions will work with the DynamoDB tables that are created as part of the stack. However, we don't set the names of the tables in the Properties resource, so they need to be generated during stack creation.

How, then, can we let our application know which table to connect to? We can do so via the environment variables in our template!

7. Let's add environment variables to the `Globals` section:

template.yaml

```yaml
Globals:
  Function:
    Timeout: 30
    Runtime: python3.8
    Handler: app.lambda_handler
    Environment:
      Variables:
        PARTIES_TABLE: !Ref PartiesTable
        GUESTS_TABLE: !Ref GuestsTable
        REPORTS_BUCKET: !Ref ReportsBucket
```

These properties will be inherited by both Lambda functions (`Registration` and `Reporting`), so we don't need to duplicate these in the resources' definitions.

There is one more thing we can do. We can create an event that we will use to test our deployment. We can also use it to test local invocations in the future.

8. Let's create a simple dummy event:

events/event.json

```json
{
    "PartyName": "Birthday",
    "PartyDate": "2020-01-01",
    "GuestName": "John Doe",
    "GuestDiet": "Vegan"
}
```

We will use this event later once we have created our application stack.

9. Let's build, package, and deploy our application:

```
$ sam build \
    --use-container
```

```
$ sam package  \
        --s3-bucket mastering-cfn-sam-bucket \
        --output-template-file template-out.yaml

$ sam deploy \
        --template-file template-out.yaml \
        --stack-name party \
        --capabilities CAPABILITY_IAM
```

10. We will check whether our function performs correctly by running a simple curl:

```
curl -X POST \
     -d @events/event.json \
     -H "Content-Type: application/json" \
     # Your API URL might differ
     https://tzsewdylmj.execute-api.eu-central-1.
amazonaws.com/Prod/register
```

We get nothing in response because our function only returns a 200 OK HTTP code.

To check the results, we will go to the DynamoDB console and examine the items:

Figure 10.5 – The DynamoDb console

The new party is also added to the **PartiesTable**:

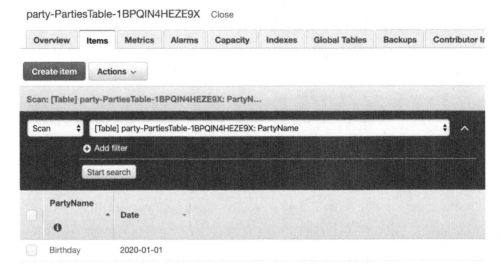

Figure 10.6 – The DynamoDB console

11. The last thing to test is running a second function. This is a scheduled task, so we will have to invoke it manually:

```
$ aws lambda invoke \
    # Your function will have a different name!
    --function-name party-ReportingFunction-
17431GZNIJXPE\
    --payload '{}' \
    out.txt
{
    "StatusCode": 200,
    "ExecutedVersion": "$LATEST"
}
```

The response shows that there were no unhandled exceptions during execution, which is a good sign!

Let's examine the file, which was uploaded to S3:

```
$ aws s3 ls \
    # Your bucket name will be different!
    s3://party-reportsbucket-1usezdtprgt9z
```

```
2020-02-19 19:58:42            124 Birthday.txt
$ aws s3 cp \
       s3://party-reportsbucket-1usezdtprgt9z/Birthday.txt
.
$ cat Birthday.txt
---
Party Planning Report!!!
Prepare for Birthday on 2021-01-01!
Guests list:
- John Doe who is restricted to eat Vegan
---
```

This shows the exact output of the data we've just stored on DynamoDB!

We have just successfully deployed and ran a serverless application consisting of multiple Lambda functions, using SAM as an all-in-one tool!

Summary

In this chapter, we learned about AWS SAM—an easy-to-use extension of CloudFormation designed specifically for serverless applications. We learned about SAM, how it differs from CloudFormation, and what it consists of.

We learned about the structure of SAM projects, deployment and operability options, and how to develop simple and complex serverless applications. This knowledge will help you to understand whether you want to start using SAM for specific projects or applications or whether you want to stick to CloudFormation.

This is the last *technical* chapter of this book. You did a great job and I hope you've learned a lot from this book and will use this knowledge to build production-ready, scalable solutions on AWS using CloudFormation.

In the next chapter, we will sit back, relax, and try to find out what we can expect from CloudFormation and IaC as a whole.

Stay tuned!

Questions

1. Is it possible to create resources that are not part of a SAM reference?

2. Which command starts a local API gateway?

3. Is it possible to delete a SAM stack using the SAM CLI?

4. Is it possible to create a sort key in a DynamoDB table using SAM?

5. What happens when you run `sam package`?

Further reading

- Comparing SAM with the Serverless Framework: `https://sanderknape.com/2018/02/comparing-aws-sam-with-serverless-framework/`

- Example SAM applications: `https://github.com/aws-samples/serverless-app-examples`

- Jeff Barr's blog post on SAM: `https://aws.amazon.com/blogs/aws/aws-serverless-application-model-sam-command-line-interface-build-test-and-debug-serverless-apps-locally/`

11
What's Next?

Welcome to the last chapter of *Mastering AWS CloudFormation*!

In this chapter, we are going to sit back and relax, since we have done a lot of hard work learning CloudFormation, its capabilities, features, and extensions. This chapter will give us an insight into what we can expect in the future for both CloudFormation and infrastructure as code.

You may wonder why we are finishing this book by making predictions when you are probably interested in continuing to practice using CloudFormation.

You may be right in that matter. This book is meant to help you master CloudFormation, and you have been busy doing this for 10 long chapters. But there is one thing you need to consider.

The world is continually changing, and so is IT, development, cloud providers, and AWS. We cannot be completely ready for what is going to happen, but we can try to predict it. In the end, it is not only technical skills but also erudition and mindset that make a good engineer.

What we will do is try to learn about the following topics:

- The future of infrastructure as code
- Understanding the difference between Terraform and CloudFormation
- Understanding the value of Cloud Development Kit

The future of infrastructure as code

Before we can foresee the future, we need to understand the past.

The term *infrastructure as code* is not new. Its roots are deep in the '90s, when sysadmins used Perl and Shell scripts to automate their regular routines. Sysadmins were the same as developers, but with a different focus (mostly automation and the stability of their infrastructure).

This focus started to shift as soon as Amazon Web Services was launched in 2006, and it became a matter of a few minutes to have a fleet of virtual machines at your disposal. The increased speed of provisioning introduced the issue of scaling performance.

In addition, it was hard to develop your own infrastructure management tools using high-level programming languages. In the end, configuration-management tools started to appear: Chef, Puppet, Ansible, and so on.

Later on, idempotence and declarable infrastructure became necessary requirements. Configuration-management tools *could* provide a state of the infrastructure, but scaling them from tens to hundreds to thousands of managed machines was hard, and these systems couldn't handle the load.

Engineers also wanted to combine resource provisioning and configuration management. CloudFormation was released in 2011 and was the first tool that was able to do both. It was a complex system, but it changed the way we implemented operations and infrastructure deployment. Instead of creating service requests or clicking through the AWS console, you could simply write a JSON template and provision the whole infrastructure.

Later in 2014, HashiCorp introduced CloudFormation's competitor—*Terraform*. Terraform offered a different approach and the support of multiple cloud providers, such as GCP and Azure. Another so called *killer feature* was its ability to create providers, software programs that acted as an interface between Terraform and service providers.

Terraform used its own **domain-specific language (DSL)** called **HashiCorp Configuration Language (HCL)**. Its syntax was similar to JSON but was simpler to read and review.

CloudFormation and Terraform followed different paths, and we will review this in the next section, but for now we need to stick to the story.

As cloud service provider have grown and developed, the term *infrastructure* has increasingly lost its original meaning. Infrastructure is no longer a bunch of virtual machines or databases: it is something that acts as a fundamental basis for software business and products.

Applying infrastructure as code in more and more services and integrating it with the **software development life cycle (SDLC)** introduced another set of problems.

What is a *build artifact*? Is it an end-product of the infrastructure as code? Is it a declaration file, which instructs a service provider to launch specific resources? Is it a framework? Or is it a state of the infrastructure with necessary resources and endpoints provided?

If so, what is the *code* part of it? How do we apply common software engineering practices to it, such as unit and integration testing? How can we make sure that the change in the infrastructure doesn't break the application?

Moreover, can we integrate the application of software with infrastructure? Can we actually combine them as a single piece of software?

Various platforms, such as *Kubernetes*, offer an opportunity to combine the application's infrastructure (or its reference) together with the source code, while the underlying infrastructure is self-managed and doesn't require that much attention.

Infrastructure has evolved from *just virtual machines* in the internet to infrastructure, platform, and software as a service. Now you can simply order a compute, storage, or any other unit and receive an endpoint to work with. For example, instead of creating a NoSQL database, you can create a DynamoDB table and work with it immediately without thinking about the underlying infrastructure, redundancy, and performance.

At this level of abstraction, we start noticing that there is not much of a difference between an application (for example, a piece of software) and the underlying infrastructure. Could this mean we can start combining them?

Let's look at this pseudocode:

```
from infrastructure import network, database, compute
from application import Application
import source_code


# Declare infrastructure to run application on
net = network.new(cidr="10.0.0.0/16",
                  subnets=3,
                  mask=24)
db = database.new(engine="mysql",
                  cpu=2,
                  mem=2048,
                  network=net)
```

```
node_cluster = compute.vm_cluster.new(count=3,
                                      cpu=2,
                                      mem=2048,
                                      network=net)


# Declare application and attach to an infrastructure
app = Application.new()
app.use_db(db)
app.run_on(node_cluster)
app.build.from_source(source_code)
```

What this code would do (if it existed) is connect to a cloud environment, create everything we've declared it to use, and then build and deploy an application on it.

Even though we can combine an actual application and the infrastructure in the same piece of code, we still have the question of the engineering roles. Who are operations, then? Software engineers? System engineers? DevOps engineers? Site-reliability engineers?

It is certain that the classic silo model, where developers and operations worked in different responsibility zones and had different priorities, is now fading away. Nowadays, we have developers, who have a good understanding of operating systems and computer networks, and we have system engineers, who code.

The industry is shifting towards convergence and there is a high chance that infrastructure as code will become simply **code**.

But we are not there yet. And before you continue your journey in cloud automation, I want you to compare two competitors—CloudFormation and Terraform—and understand their differences. Learning this will help you to make a proper decision for your particular case, current or future.

Understanding the difference between Terraform and CloudFormation

First of all, we are not evaluating CloudFormation and Terraform to find the best infrastructure-as-code instrument on the market. Our goal is to find a tool that fits the purpose and our use case (whatever it is going to be).

We are going to look at the following features:

- Provider support
- Declaration syntax
- Development and deployment methodologies

Let's start with provider support.

Provider support

CloudFormation as an invention of Amazon Web Services originally supported itself as the only service provider.

Terraform was developed as a *cloud-agnostic* tool, meaning that it could communicate with various cloud and service providers, thus making it one tool to rule them all.

This concept was made available with the use of providers—specific abstractions that handle communication between a service provider and Terraform. Providers are written in the same language as Terraform (for example, Golang) and can be used locally (if you ever need to create your own provider for specific purpose) or distributed via OpenSource and submitted to HashiCorp via a special form.

Terraform has a big variety of providers, both developed by vendors (`https://www.terraform.io/docs/providers/index.html`) and community (`https://www.terraform.io/docs/providers/type/community-index.html`). HashiCorp heavily invested in building framework and wrappers in order to make provider development doable for everyone.

On the one hand, Terraform's success as a universal infrastructure-as-code instrument leaves no chance for its competitors from major cloud providers: AWS CloudFormation, Azure Resource Manager, and Google Cloud Deployment Manager. On the other hand, Terraform heavily relies on the speed of these providers' development—it is obvious that cloud providers' tools will be the first to support the newest services and API changes. In addition to that, the engineer has to take care of backward compatibility, as a new version of a provider may not work with an old version of the resource declaration in the template.

However, the ability to create external resources (for example, outside of AWS) is desirable. Although custom resources (CRs) allow us to do that, it is hard to properly organize them at scale. Imagine creating CRs for GCP so that you can create resources in GCP using CloudFormation.

The CloudFormation development team came up with a centralized solution for this problem. A new feature called CloudFormation Registry allows us to create your own resource providers—in a similar manner to Terraform—using not only Go, but also Java (generally available) and Python (in developer preview at the time of writing)!

CloudFormation Registry is outside the scope of this book because an AWS engineer most likely won't need to create their own provider; however, service providers, such as Atlassian, Datadog, New Relic, SpotInst, and others, are already onboarding. CloudFormation will most likely compete soon with Terraform in its variety of supported vendors.

Let's continue our journey and look at the syntax differences.

Declaration syntax

We know that CloudFormation templates are written in JSON or YAML, depending on the developer's preference. The declaration of CloudFormation is a key–value block, where the key is a logical name of the resource and the value is its attributes, such as type and properties.

The following code shows the resource declaration of a CloudFormation resource:

```
MyResourceLogicalName:
  Type: AWS::Service::ResourceType
  Properties:
    PropertyA: some value
    PropertyB: some value
    # and so on
```

This declaration makes it easy to reference resource identifiers in the declaration using functions such as `Fn::Sub`, `Fn::Ref`, and `Fn::GetAtt`.

Terraform has its own **domain-specific language** called **HashiCorp Configuration Language (HCL)**. HCL is a JSON-like language with a small bit of syntax sugar on top.

Let's say we want to create a VPC and a subnet in AWS using Terraform. Our template file would look like the following:

```
resource "aws_vpc" "vpc" {
  cidr_block = "10.0.0.0/16"
}
resource "aws_subnet" "subnet" {
  vpc_id     = "${aws_vpc.vpc.id}"
```

```
    cidr_block = "10.0.1.0/24"
}
```

As you can see, there are huge differences.

The actual type of the resource is the first string after the keyword resource, followed by the logical name (`resource "RESOURCE_TYPE" "LOGICAL_NAME" {}`), while in CloudFormation, we have the logical name of the resource followed by the type in a separate field.

The second difference is that we need to provide a resource type, logical name, and attribute (`"${aws_vpc.vpc.id}"`) so that we can refer to it in another resource, since Terraform doesn't support any default return values such as CloudFormation and `Fn::Ref`.

There are many other differences, such as iterations and conditions in HCL, which are used to grant the ability to provide the same features that are already supported by CloudFormation, but that's not our main focus for now.

Now let's look at the last, but not least, thing that we should learn about—deployment and development. Let's dive in.

Development and deployment methodologies

CloudFormation is flexible for development. An AWS engineer can use nested stacks or a cross-stack resource reference using *exports* and `Fn::ImportValue` to manage each piece of infrastructure independently. The huge variety and agility of intrinsic functions allows AWS engineers to create reusable templates.

When it comes to deployments and stack operations, CloudFormation has it all. ChangeSets allow granular control over stack updates, yet the `aws cloudformation deploy` command makes it simple to create a continuous delivery pipeline for both new and existing stacks.

CloudFormation has a lot of capabilities for various cases, as shown in the following list:

- For large-scale infrastructure or products, there are StackSets.
- For customization, there are template macros and custom resources.
- For configuration management, there is *cfn-init*.
- For provisioning security, there are CloudFormation service roles.
- In case of failure, there is one of the most important and useful features of CloudFormation, automatic and seamless rollbacks.

Amazon Web Services did a great job by making CloudFormation suit any type of company, running its applications and systems on AWS.

Terraform follows a different path. It does not focus on a single cloud—instead, it tries to support as many cloud providers, third-party services, and even external systems as it can.

You can use known configuration-management systems, such as Ansible, Puppet, Chef, and SaltStack, with Terraform using provisioners, which will save a lot of time if you used them for your on-premise infrastructure and are now moving to the cloud. Terraform is able to retrieve information from the provider via its API using *data*, for example, it can call AWS's API to obtain the ID of an already existing VPC and use it to create subnets.

Terraform does not support rollbacks, so you have to rely on its state file backup—which is stored locally or remotely—if things go nasty.

This said, it is up to you—the engineer—to make the decision as to whether you want to use Terraform or CloudFormation. If you feel comfortable with YAML and JSON and plan to work only with AWS, then choose CloudFormation. If you are looking for a vendor-agnostic tool with tens of services and the support from the open source community, then you might want to look at Terraform.

This chapter is not only about using declarative language to define infrastructure. In the next section, we are going to look at their potential successors and what value they deliver to everybody in IT.

Understanding the value of Cloud Development Kit

DSL-based instruments, such as CloudFormation and Terraform, are still the standard of infrastructure as code. They are well known, have a huge community worldwide, and keep developing.

However, they also have several problems that its successor, CDK, is able to solve.

In this section, we are going to take a sneak peek at what changes and value CDK is bringing to the industry.

We will start by looking at the testing capabilities, since this was one of the main headaches with infrastructure as code.

Testing infrastructure

In order to test a computer program, all we need to do is build it, and then run some written test scenarios. The expected behavior of the software is known, so all you need is to receive the proper result.

In *Chapter 4, Continuous Integration and Deployment*, we did this with CloudFormation by deploying our infrastructure and running specific infrastructure tests on it. For declarative tools, this is the only working way we have of testing them, but spinning up separate infrastructure for tests is a long and, in some cases, very expensive process. In some situations it is even impossible.

This is mainly because the way the resources are declared in templates doesn't mean that the service provider will be able to process that information. For example, CloudFormation cannot tell whether we have supplied the correct AMI ID for the EC2 instance. Also, Kubernetes cannot tell whether a Docker image exists when we write a pod declaration.

The lack of testing support was also due to the ambiguity around what was being tested. What do we need to test? That the resource will be created? That the resource will be created *exactly* as we declared it? Why should it not?

However, what should always be tested is integration. In massive projects and infrastructures, we don't only care about a small network with a bunch of machines in it. There are hundreds and thousands of compute, storage, transport, analytics, and other resources, all of them developed and provisioned by different teams.

CDK offers a different way to create infrastructure. Instead of writing a declarative instruction on what to create, we write a computer program using the **object-oriented programming** (**OOP**) paradigm. Each resource is a class that has relations with other classes. VPC is a class. Subnet is a class that is related to VPC. The RDS database subnet group is a class that relates to a subnet.

These relations are declared programmatically, and moreover, the CDK is a framework for a programming language. This means that you are not writing a template—you are literally writing a piece of software!

This allows you to run complex testing against it, using the best practices from the software engineering world. And all this without spending even a single penny on creating tens or hundreds of resources to check this!

And testing is not the only thing we can do with the help of CDK. What about combining the application with the infrastructure?

Adding artifacts

When we use pure CloudFormation, we cannot add artifacts to it, simply because CloudFormation is a system for provisioning infrastructure and resources, something that our application will run on. Support for adding an application to the stack was partially added with `cfn-init`. With the serverless application model, it was possible to have all-in-one source code with an infrastructure template, but that only works for applications based on AWS Lambda.

CDK is not just a framework that generates CloudFormation templates—it comes with many abstractions on top of it.

One of these abstractions is **assets**, CDK constructs that are used to bundle the application artifact, whether it's a binary or a ZIP file, a directory, or a Docker image.

Imagine that you have a project structure with your source code in the `foo` directory. This directory also contains a Dockerfile, which is built and pushed to the AWS ECR repository.

In this case, we can use assets to bundle and include the image in our infrastructure, as shown in the following example:

```python
import aws_cdk.aws_ecs as ecs
from aws_cdk.aws_ecr_assets import DockerImageAsset
# Declare Asset object with a path to app
asset = DockerImageAsset(self,
                         "image",
                         directory="/path/to/foo")
# Declare Task Definition
td = ecs.FargateTaskDefinition(self,
                               "td",
                               memory_limit_mib=512,
                               cpu=256)
# Add container built from the Asset image to Task Definition
td.add_container("container",image=ecs.ContainerImage.
fromEcrRepository(asset.repository,
        asset.image_uri))
```

What this code is doing is that it builds and pushes the Docker image with the source code of the original application and sends it to the ECR repository. It then creates an ECS task definition with a container definition, pointing to the ECR image URI as a source.

This abstraction allows us to literally mix our applications with the infrastructure, managing them as a whole! And since CDK is a multilingual project, more and more products and projects can be built with this, without forcing the developer to learn additional languages (which is still a nice skill to have and do).

CDK is only at the start of its journey, but its future is promising and game changing. It may not replace CloudFormation (such a system simply cannot be replaced), but sooner or later, it will act as the translation mechanism between a code written by developers and an actual working and serving infrastructure.

Summary

In this chapter, we learned about what we can expect in the future. First, we looked into the past and the future of infrastructure—what is changing and what these changes mean to us as AWS professionals. Then we defined the main differences between CloudFormation and its biggest competitor, Terraform, and why these two systems follow such different paths. At the end of the chapter, we looked into the actual value that CDK brings us.

With this in mind, you should be able to understand where to go next in your journey. Will you want to keep mastering CloudFormation? After this book, the only information you will need is found in CloudFormation's documentation. CloudFormation's development team is working hard to develop and evolve their product, so spend some time reviewing their coverage roadmap and public repository with tons of useful information.

Will you want to start practicing software development? If so, CDK is a good start for you.

I wish you all the best in this journey. Let's see where it will take us!

Further reading

- AWS's blog on the CloudFormation Registry: `https://aws.amazon.com/blogs/aws/cloudformation-update-cli-third-party-resource-support-registry/`

- AWS CloudFormation GitHub project: `https://github.com/aws-cloudformation`

- AWS CloudFormation coverage roadmap: `https://github.com/aws-cloudformation/aws-cloudformation-coverage-roadmap`

- AWS CloudFormation awesome list: `https://github.com/aws-cloudformation/awesome-cloudformation`

Assessments

Chapter 1: CloudFormation Refresher

1. CreateStack.

2. CloudFormation Service Role is an IAM Role that is assumed by CloudFormation before stack operations are performed. The policies attached to that role will be then used to perform stack operations.

3. The ones that are attached to the IAM entity (User or Role), which run CloudFormation stack operations.

4. This information (physical resource ID and its metadata) is stored in CloudFormation's state.

5. If we try to create the same stack (that is, invoke the CreateStack API call), that call will fail with a `400 AlreadyExists` error.

6. If we run a stack update without any changes in a template or parameters, nothing would happen as there are no changes. CloudFormation will not notice if the resource has been deleted manually. But if we update the deleted resource, the operation will fail, because the CloudFormation resource still exists in the state and CloudFormation *believes* it is still there.

7. Because CloudFormation's state is immutable and cannot be managed by the end user. In order to recreate the deleted resource we have to delete it from the state by deleting it from the template, and then add it again.

Chapter 2: Advanced Template Development

1. No. The `Condition` attribute of the resource may have only the `Condition` name string format.

2. Yes, it is possible to use `Fn::Ref`, `Fn::GetAttr` or other relevant intrinsic functions with conditional functions such as `Fn::If`.

3. `UpdatePolicy` is a resource attribute that handles the updates for resources such as the Auto Scaling group. `UpdateReplacePolicy` is used to manage the behavior of resources that are being replaced by CloudFormation during stack operations.

4. Retain, since we cannot afford to delete mission-critical databases by mistake in a template or stack operation.

5. `Fn::ImportValue` take the values of exported outputs of other stacks.

6. Yes, but not in the same AWS Region.

7. Yes, there is an AWS-specific parameter type called `AWS::EC2::Image::Id`.

8. `AWS::NoValue` can be referred to a null value. It is not usually used to set any value to a resource property and is mostly used in conjunction with conditional functions.

Chapter 3: Validation, Linting, and Deployment of the Stack

1. From 9,000 and above.

2. Linting is the process of evaluating the template against linter rules and is performed by `cfn-lint`. Validation is performed by CloudFormation and checks whether the template is valid and can be processed by CloudFormation.

3. There are several steps:

    (a) CloudFormation will check whether the stack exists or not.

    (b) CloudFormation will create a ChangeSet for a new or existing stack.

    (c) CloudFormation will execute the ChangeSet and listen to the stack events.

    (d) If there is a failure, CloudFormation rolls back the changes and informs the user about the issue.

4. No, ChangeSets must have unique names, otherwise you will get a `400 AlreadyExists` error.

5. The name of the rule file and the rule class must be the same.

6. Just add the necessary change to the template or parameters and run the stack update.

Chapter 4: Continuous Integration and Deployment

1. `buildspec.yml` is a build specification file with instructions for AWS CodeBuild on how to process the build.

2. A CloudFormation artifact is the template and, for some cases, parameter files. They are stored on S3.

3. You can use CloudFormation signals, wait conditions, and update policies.

4. `ListStackResources`.

5. Source, Build, and Deploy. There are various services that can be used, such as S3, CodeBuild, CodeDeploy, and CloudFormation.

Chapter 5: Deploying to Multiple Regions and Accounts Using StackSets

1. Yes, but it is not recommended. You will have to then explicitly specify the names of both roles.

2. Yes, this is managed by a property called *Maximum Concurrent Accounts*.

3. Per Region (as they are defined from the first to last) and then per account (as they are defined from the first to last).

4. No, you must delete all the stack instances first.

5. The only action for the Administrator role is to assume the Execution role.

Chapter 6: Configuration Management of the EC2 Instances Using cfn-init

1. The `cfn-init` helper script processes these configuration sections in the following order: packages, groups, users, sources, files, commands, and then services. Yes, and it is recommended to do so for complex configurations or to run configuration items in a different order.

2. No.

3. Not using the `files` directive in the config set. You will have to use the `commands` directive, but it is possible to add a missing directory to the full path of the file, and `cfn-init` will automatically create it (similar to the `mkdir -p` command).

4. `WaitCondition` is a CloudFormation resource that is used to make CloudFormation wait for resource completion. For example, you can use `WaitCondition` with `cfn-signal` to make CloudFormation inform the users about resource creation only when `cfn-init` has finished running.

Chapter 7: Creating Resources outside AWS Using Custom Resources

1. Create, Update, and Delete.

2. Only using Lambda Layers. Or simply copy the module content to the Lambda function's code.

3. CloudFormation as a requester, AWS Lambda for provisioning, CloudWatch for logs and metrics, and other AWS services, if they are used in the custom resource's logic.

4. `responseReason`.

5. The event is an actual payload to the Lambda function, which has to be processed. Context is metadata of the Lambda request that contains various information, such as the timestamp of request.

Chapter 8: Dynamically Rendering the Template Using Template Macros

1. JSON. It is either a piece of a template or a full template, depending on whether the `Transform` section is declared or the `Fn::Transform` function is being used.

2. No, because a macro and its function must be in the same Region.

3. The stack operation will be considered as Failed and CloudFormation will start rolling back.

4. Yes, but you need to be aware of the macro evaluation order (`https://docs.aws.amazon.com/AWSCloudFormation/latest/UserGuide/template-macros.html#template-macros-use`).

Chapter 9: Generating CloudFormation Templates Using AWS CDK

1. Constructs are building blocks of CDK. Any block of CDK, such as App, Stack, Asset, or Resource is considered to be a Construct.

2. You have to define each stack separately by assigning a stack class to it as a value.

3. By adding subnet configuration to the VPC construct. Originally, CDK was developed by TypeScript, but there are libraries for Python, Java, C#, and JavaScript. The CDK development team is working on more languages to support in CDK.

4. No, CDK will use the default credentials and config to connect to AWS. But it is recommended to provide an account ID and Region when using CDK in production.

Chapter 10: Deploying Serverless Applications Using AWS SAM

1. Yes, by using CloudFormation-specific resource types.

2. `sam local start-api`.

3. No, SAM CLI doesn't have this command. You will have to use AWS CLI to delete the stack (`aws cloudformation delete-stack`).

4. It is, but you have to use the CloudFormation-specific type for DynamoDB, since `SimpleTable` doesn't have this property.

5. The application's source code and its dependencies are uploaded to S3 as a ZIP file. The template is altered to point to S3 for the source code and is saved on disk or printed to the Terminal output.

Other Books You May Enjoy

If you enjoyed this book, you may be interested in these other books by Packt:

AWS Security Cookbook

Heartin Kanikathottu

ISBN: 978-1-83882-625-3

- Create and manage users, groups, roles, and policies across accounts
- Use AWS Managed Services for logging, monitoring, and auditing
- Check compliance with AWS Managed Services that use machine learning
- Provide security and availability for EC2 instances and applications
- Secure data using symmetric and asymmetric encryption
- Manage user pools and identity pools with federated login

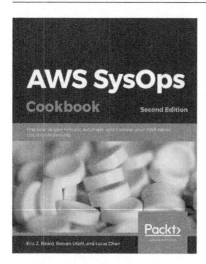

AWS SysOps Cookbook - Second Edition

Eric Z. Beard, Rowan Udell, Et al

ISBN: 978-1-83855-018-9

- Secure your account by creating IAM users and avoiding the use of the root login
- Simplify the creation of a multi-account landing zone using AWS Control Tower
- Master Amazon S3 for unlimited, cost-efficient storage of data
- Explore a variety of compute resources on the AWS Cloud, such as EC2 and AWS Lambda
- Configure secure networks using Amazon VPC, access control lists, and security groups
- Estimate your monthly bill by using cost estimation tools
- Learn to host a website with Amazon Route 53, Amazon CloudFront, and S3

Leave a review - let other readers know what you think

Please share your thoughts on this book with others by leaving a review on the site that you bought it from. If you purchased the book from Amazon, please leave us an honest review on this book's Amazon page. This is vital so that other potential readers can see and use your unbiased opinion to make purchasing decisions, we can understand what our customers think about our products, and our authors can see your feedback on the title that they have worked with Packt to create. It will only take a few minutes of your time, but is valuable to other potential customers, our authors, and Packt. Thank you!

Index